PRAISE OF *NOT THAT SWEET*

"Stephanie's voice is soulful and vulnerable, sharing an honest glimpse into a youth of wanting and striving that so many of us can relate to. Her evolution in her attachment to herself is raw and resonant. These pages remind us all that we are always enough and never too much."

Dr. Han Ren, Licensed Psychologist, Author of *The Hyphenated Life* **(in press)**

"An intimate look into the complex, and often confusing, world of family estrangement and surviving abuse. With attentive honesty, Stephanie Thoma invites the reader to see the one we lost first was ourselves, and by untangling our history's threads we can release the lies we were told about who we are and reclaim our identity from the impossible demand of being good. *Not That Sweet* is a journal entry witness to every scapegoat's experience and welcome home to their tender, wild, and authentic self."

Katherine Sleadd, Author of *How to Be a Bad Friend*

"*Not That Sweet* is a fierce and empowering narrative that dives headfirst into the complexities of family relationships and the journey to reclaiming our identities after surviving abuse. With her unapologetic honesty, Stephanie Thoma challenges us to confront the lies we've been told and step into our personal power. This book is a bold call to embrace our authentic selves, serving as a compassionate guide for anyone navigating their own journey. If you're ready for a profound exploration of truth and healing, this is an absolute must-read!"

Vasavi Kumar, Author of *Say It Out Loud*

"*Not That Sweet* is a profound exploration of family estrangement and forging your own identity through rejection, acceptance, holding on, letting go, and moving on. Each story Stephanie Thoma shares is moving—you'll find yourself catching your breath, laughing, exclaiming, and crying. This poignant and powerful narrative is not just a riveting book; it's like the perfect confidante for anyone working to reclaim themselves from complicated shadows of the past.

A must-read for those ready, or working to embrace their authentic selves!"

Gabrielle Stanley Blair, Author of *Ejaculate Responsibly*

"*Not That Sweet* is a powerful, honest account of the complicated family dynamics that can encourage us to look deep within, muster courage, and seek out our own mirrors in the world. Stephanie Thoma's first-hand account portrays how hard we can try to find belonging, love and acceptance within our families, and still come up short. Filled with personal, ambiguous losses, and disenfranchised grief, striving to navigate the world, find the right support, and see ourselves as we truly are: worthy of love and belonging. This book serves as a catalyst for opening the conversation on self-compassion, determination, and the painful, but necessary choices we make - this is so deeply needed."

Gina Moffa, LCSW, Trauma and Grief Therapist and Author of *Moving On Doesn't Mean Letting Go*

NOT THAT SWEET

Stephanie Thoma

Copyright © 2024 by Stephanie Thoma

All rights reserved. No part of this book may be used or reproduced by any means, graphic, electronic, or mechanical, including photocopying, recording, taping, or by any information storage retrieval system, without the written permission of the publisher.

All names have been changed for privacy. Views expressed in this book are as accurate as possible to the observed and lived perspective of the characters at the time, as recalled or recorded. The circumstances and thoughts shared across this timeline do not necessarily reflect what feels true or persists today.

ISBN: 978-1-952802-02-7 (ebook)

ISBN: 978-1-952802-03-4 (paperback)

Cover design by Jelena Gajic @coverbookdesigns

Photo on back cover by Meg Marie McMillan

"To know and be yourself is the greatest power. To be seen and celebrated is the greatest love." - Stephanie Thoma, CHt

For every underdog, tall poppy, scapegoat, black sheep, or outlier, who dares to live a life true to themselves.

CONTENTS

PREFACE vii

1. FAMILY TIES 1

2. FIRST LOVE 40

3. BOARDING SCHOOL 79

4. YOUTH SHELTER 105

5. JUVENILE HALL 107

6. MENTAL HOSPITAL 126

7. ORIGINS 147

8. STEP RIGHT UP 172

CONCLUSION 175

BOOK CLUB QUESTIONS 179

CONTACT 183

ACKNOWLEDGEMENTS 184

ABOUT THE AUTHOR 186

PREFACE

I have a question for you: Would you rather live a life that's good or interesting?

It may sound like a trick question — can't we have both?

But if you're like me, you do your best to embrace the light and the dark as the contrast that helps you know up from down.

If you're new to my work, this may feel like an intimate introduction. And by you reading this, I can assume I have your consent as we dive into some origin storytelling. My intention is not to trauma-dump on you, but to share some of my sharpest and softest memories that have a broader meaning both standing alone and when woven together. In my story, may you find glimpses of your own, as we strive to sort through our personal experiences, making every effort to soften our understanding of ourselves, as well as the lives of those we observe each day. Each fragment and moment was written and recalled to the best of my ability, with names changed for privacy. I have taken care to go off of mostly memory and journal entries to populate the stories shared here. And may sparingly make a few direct quotes.

Let's start with the most recent events at the time of your reading.

1. FAMILY TIES

2012 - 2023

"She knows her truth and she leads herself."

-"Villainize" by Stephanie Thoma

2012, age 21, Novato, CA

"I'd like to be matched with the toughest case you have. The girl who people turn away because she is too difficult," I tell the YMCA youth mentor team during my phone interview.

Becoming an official mentor like the one I had over a decade ago was not a long-term ambition, but now that it's possible, it's an intuitive, unfaltering, "yes."

If I can provide help in the same way I once received it, that will feel like magic. I'll show myself how far I have come. I can be exactly who I really am, defying all of the projections about me that were plain wrong. There is heart in this, and also some ego. It's taking ownership of my self-concept and getting to impact a life — the proof is in the pudding there. I will be present, loyal, and make the role of mentor my own by being honest and frank and kind.

What a privilege to get to be her one and only mentor. It's not a duty I take lightly. I choose her and she gets to choose me.

I vow to always listen non-judgmentally, remember special details about her likes and dislikes, provide guidance when she is open to it, and earn that openness by facilitating fun activities for us like grabbing ice cream, going on walks, to the playground, and being upbeat, present, and making it fun no matter what we do. This is the epitome of creating yourself — something that she may not yet realize she can do too. I apply and go through the whole process before they realize I am too young. You have to be twenty-three to be a mentor, so we postpone the final steps.

2014, age 23, Novato, CA

"Have you tried smiling when you go up to ask someone to play?" I ask in a curious and light-hearted way.

My mentee is twelve but developmentally six, and going through puberty with minimal social skills. We go to playgrounds, and when approaching other kids, usually several years younger, she speaks in a monotone with a straight face. We go over how to smile and lift one's tone when talking, and it makes a difference. She doesn't like it when I come over because of our "no tech" rule. She is always playing video games, six to twelve hours a day, likely because it occupies her while her parents go about their day. I knew it was necessary to have those few hours of interacting face to face with me, but she resisted it.

We meet weekly and go to parks, creameries, ice cream shops and trails, and there are times when she lashes out with name-calling, and I set boundaries, but not without asking her, "How could someone feel when you say that to them?"

I can see her improving, smiling at people, taking initiative to socialize, but do not extend to an additional year because navigating her fits of anger feel like a lot for me to handle as I try to stay strong in so many other areas of my life. Being a martyr is no accomplishment, and I knew I had honored my year-long commitment and planted seeds and she is better off because of our time together, even if her mom would have preferred that I extend.

During our last week, she exclaims, "I got another Stephanie mentor."

I can tell that is how this family dynamic works; a bit detached, switching one out for another, sort of like my parents with my dogs growing up, new dog, same name, after one had passed. But the seeds planted will sprout, and I don't need to be there or have anything attributed to our work together to know that truth.

I know I cannot be replaced and believe deep down she knows too, but it's not about that. I remind myself: I do things with intention, and check-in, but ultimately have no control over how much something means to someone else. Although we do not stay connected, I recall moments of her looking at me fondly, experiencing the simple joys of a picnic at the Petaluma Cheese Company, an assortment of the ones she liked best laid out atop the special multi-use fold-up blanket I got for occasions like these. She doesn't always express gratitude with her words, but the softness of her smile and the glimmer in her eye let me know we are building new pathways for her to experience the world through, and I'm doing this for myself as much as her. We can't do things while being of service without acknowledging what we have to gain, even intangibly. We are all works of art in progress.

2016, age 25, San Francisco, CA

The letter. I write it during my last week of being twenty-five-years-old while on a commuter ferry connecting San Francisco with Marin County. A quarter of a century of life lived approaches and I try to console the hurt that I can sense under the surface of my heart. A tiny ache that was once so strong, now subdued, since it doesn't make sense to listen to. I need to keep moving forward, and in terms of physical distance, I have managed to create more space between myself and my family. Being away from home in the city comes with a sense of guilt, of not visiting enough. I am on a ferry ride home for a random summer weekend, and I am not excited. I feel a sense of cool calm grounding my body, and my mind is contemplative.

I recall the paint set I gave my dad last year, after years of noticing some paintings in the shed he declared he made himself (with some help with paint-by-numbers). But even so, not everyone can evoke soul in each colorful stroke, within the lines but with another intangible quality to it, like he had. Usually sad clowns with puddly brown eyes and overdrawn red mouths with limp-stemmed flowers in their hats. As far as I know, he put it away as soon as I gave it to him, writing off what was once a source of connection, once an outlet, like he had written off the chance to connect more deeply with me.

How badly some people just want to move on from challenging times or challenging relationships, and discard aspects of their expression and purpose in the process. Maybe he associates it with another person, or another time, not realizing that when you find an art form, when you truly love it, you can go through periods apart, but it's a love that will always love you back. It's like with me, even if I don't sing or write a song for a while, and my voice isn't as polished, the words still flood once I get pen to paper after hearing the words-with-a-tune spontaneously come into my head.

Maybe if Dad would create art like he did when he was younger, he could find an even greater connection with himself and others. I still think he can. But as he has told me, "You can lead a horse to water, but you can't make them drink."

I write a letter to my dad acknowledging that he was physically present during my childhood, which is amazing considering that his dad wasn't. And that, of course, didn't excuse some of the ways he parented me, things he did and said, acknowledging that I was challenging, coming into the world with core beliefs that differed from his own. I trust that he did his best, and I appreciate the effort that was exercised during the chaos. I forgive him and expect nothing from him. As I look out at the water, the words that drip onto my paper feel serene; if my heart were speaking, this is exactly what it would say. A part of me still yearns to be witnessed in this soft, emotional, vulnerable place. But even I know the letter isn't truly vulnerable. It's partially agreeing, placating; yes we should all move on and you did your best as a parent. I haven't been a part of any type of abusive relationship as an adult, so that's good, right? I think my parents know deep down that I did not deserve some of that treatment, though. Not inviting in more conversation after so many rejections of it. Knowing better than to say it to his face because he'll shut down and shut me out. Maybe if I drop it off, there will be a moment, doors closed, alone in his study, where he reads my words, and maybe feels something. Feels how much I want to be loved specifically by him, and how that was a letdown, but now I am accepting it, and willing to accept the love he does have. I'll take it without judgment and with gratitude. If it's the best he can do, I'll decide that it's enough, logical reason above all else. Before my next ferry ride back to the city, I leave it with him, setting it on the table with his name, seeing him walk up to it before I head out of the door, and I suppose I'll never know what he thought about it. He doesn't reply. Luckily, that is not the point this time.

2017, age 27, Novato, CA

Visiting home for the holidays, Thanksgiving this time, doing some work in the den with my dad's book collection and the very back door, probably locked, as it always is. Even though it was 'my room' as a kid, I moved around to different rooms in the house about five times. This was my second-to-last room before they placed me in the one farthest away from everyone near the very front door. This room was my place for probably a year, which was fine, except for when my mom had bunko nights, where she and friends would get together with dice and cards and cocktails and be hooting and hollering until very late. She asked me to not leave my room, which felt like a prison sentence when I had to pee. There is also a secret room. It was my room except for a closet where there were board games and wrapping paper, and beyond that is another door with a lock on it. Since the only way to get in there was to enter my room, sometimes I would notice a desk and chair peering in as my dad was in there, door ajar. I knew better than to go in there, in his private space, but as an adult on a temporary visit, I was feeling brave.

I lock the door to what is now the entrance to the "back room" or "computer room" and make my way into the closet, my heart racing as I sift past the bags of what will probably become wrapped presents the following month. I reach for the handle to the furthest back door with trepidation and, to my amazement, it is unlocked. I walk in and notice a moldy scent, and cobwebs lining an antique desk and the walls of unpainted concrete and a furnace. Like a sort of bunker. There's a small ledge within a crevice to the left, and there I see my name, *Thoma, Stephanie* on a row of cobweb-crusted empty pill bottles. I am as curious as I am appalled. Why would he keep these? What is the purpose? When I look at the floor, stacks of black VHS tapes labeled in call caps *STEPHANIE TANTRUMS*. And I recall all the times when I would be crying loudly and my mom would come over and shove that camera in my face and I'd scream more. This was age nine or so. They were to show the 'professionals' that even though I managed my emotions outside of the home when they saw me in their offices, I was actually capable of a lot of emotion. Disturber of the peace. It was humiliating, but it wouldn't stop me. I still cried, but usually harder because I knew they didn't care what I was experiencing and just wanted proof to share with strangers. So, here it is, here is your proof.

My heart is pounding. I know I shouldn't be here. I have a solid alibi, and if anyone asks why the entrance door to the back room is locked, I'm working and need privacy, obviously. I instinctively grab the top tape and put it under my coat. I feel a surge of adrenaline and realize I cannot possibly fit all of the tapes in my coat. I also feel guilty. This is Dad's property. Even though it's remnants of me.

Later that day, I walk over to the recycling bin outside. I place the labeled tape in the bin. Part of me considers hiding it below everything. Dad often takes out the trash after all, but another part of me leaves it right there toward the top. I go to check on the trash the next day, and the tape is gone as the other trash remains. I return to Dad's back room, and once again, like before, the door to the concrete room is locked.

2018, age 27, Novato, CA

I set the boundary of visiting for Christmas only this year, no Thanksgiving. And the thought of going to everybody's birthday, eight of them if you count their German Shepherd, makes less sense to me now than it used to. I've tried to go out of my way to show my love because that's what we're supposed to do for family. Sacrifice things you'd like to do to show them you care. As my mom likes to say, "There's nothing more important than family." For years I've gone along with that value, prioritizing attending family gatherings, even more so since moving to the city that we were fifth generation residents of, San Francisco, until the move 45 minutes across the Golden Gate bridge when I was four. These days taking buses or ferries or getting rides like a carpooling Elementary schooler with Mom or Dad back to that place. "Home."

That served as the backdrop for so many trips for so many years. A tenseness in my shoulders and constriction in my throat. Saying "no" to special event invitations where I could make a new friend or create a new business opportunity, and I say "no" to those to say "yes" to this?

Why put all of your effort into something that is mediocre at best? This is my life, I remind myself. Why am I acting in accordance with a rule book that doesn't even really exist? Or take into account special circumstances? Screw what everyone says I should do. I go through phases of being "over" what happened, and then there will be times when I remember specific instances and feel sick to my stomach on the way back down that dead-end private street. The same one where I'd crouch down inside cars coming from certain places so that the neighbors my age who went to my school wouldn't see. As if they didn't already know. More on that later.

As Mother's Day rolls around, I begin to feel guilty about not going home for it, even though I set the boundary that I would not be going to most family things anymore. I *should* go. There's nothing better to do and she'll appreciate it. My dad comes to pick me up and we make that same trek and I go for a jog on an old favorite trail, one of the truest, purest pleasures of going back to that town.

When I get back, I head up to her room to see if I can surprise her. She looks at me — previously laughing and smiling — then her eyes squint and her energy lowers, "What are you doing here?"

"I thought maybe you'd want to see me. It's Mother's Day. You're my mom. Happy Mother's Day," I say in a matter-of-fact monotone, feeling myself cut off the hurt with the swiftness of a blunt knife to a cucumber, that sinking feeling of needles in my chest that was beginning drops down into my stomach and down my legs until I feel nothing.

"I'd hug you, but you're all sweaty." She sighs, eyes cast to the side.

"Really? Okay. It's your day. You don't have to hug me. I thought you'd be happy to see me."

"I would hug you, after your shower... Oh, come here." She motions for me to come closer as she forces a smile and I oblige. The hug is stiff and distanced, and as we pull away, she gets back on script. "I'm glad you're here."

We're each doing what we're supposed to. Good.

I rationalize that she is usually much warmer, but probably processing her surprise in seeing me after feeling rejected by me and coming to terms with my absence, although the hope would be a sort of unconditional loving feeling from her. That's just now how it is. I shower and read until it's time to go to brunch and then get a ride back to the city. I ask the other kids if I can sit next to her. "You all get to see her every day. You live with her. If she'd like, I'll sit here," and I do. I want to make the most of the opportunities that we have since I'm intuiting that I won't be coming back for Mother's Day again. I'll never say never, but it's certainly not looking likely.

I'm so glad my littlest sister, twenty-one-year-old Cassie, is also next to me. She strikes a balance of calling me on my shit that I usually don't think is shit, but also letting me know, "What Mom/Dad did/said was fucked up."

We walk briskly to the banquet to refill our plates several times. I'm present, until I'm not. I feel ready to leave and sit in silence as Mom converses with the other kids. I feel invisible, but it's what she wants, and maybe I want that too, today.

Luckily, my dad is ready to go as well, but not before several family pictures, per my mom's usual request. After one too many pics, my dad is already walking off to his car, Mom having driven most of us there, and I don't know where he parked. I search the parking lot and eventually find him. He's fuming. I know he's upset that I didn't find the car faster. I would have liked to have walked together for the sake of logistics, anticipating this, but I say nothing. Further confirmation that this detachment is healthy. We head back home as my mom and other siblings take their time heading to the van. I have plans to meet up with a friend before I leave, and am looking forward to the sun and friend that I've missed. We have some time at the pool before it's close to getting dark, and time for me to leave this place and go back to San Francisco.

"Do you want me to stay for a family dinner?" I ask after my friend leaves.

"No," my dad says. "I'm going to take you home now before it's dark."

He blasts a sports game after telling me a story from that week that he told me on the initial car ride that morning as though it's the first time. How he's starting to catch eels as a pastime. He goes under the Golden Gate bridge by himself and catches them with his bare hands and slipped on a rock while carrying the bucket with waves crashing over him.

"Dad, don't you think you should go with someone for safety?" I have a feeling he gets a thrill out of it and wouldn't half mind if it was the end of him.

"No. Now let me finish the story…" It would be a story to tell, he'd rationalize, even if he wouldn't be the one to tell it. It could be a legacy of sorts. I listen and that's all he needs. When we're close to home, I pull out his Father's Day gift. "I wanted to give you your gift early, before you go. You're welcome to open it now."

He grabs the bag and throws it in the backseat.

"Why don't you feel comfortable opening it now?" I ask in a soft, curious tone.

"I'm afraid I might cry," he says without flinching, and I have no idea if he's kidding or not.

We park in front of a burrito place. "Do you want a burrito?" he asks. It'll be like the Father's Day dinner we will not be having this year, I rationalize as I follow behind him.

We enter the restaurant across the street from my apartment as they're closing.

"Do you want to get the burritos to go and have them at my place?" I offer.

"Woah, woah." His face is getting red, and his body tenses as his head violently shakes side-to-side. "If I knew you weren't going to eat with me at that table [points to the right] then I wouldn't have come here."

Before my own emotions can kick in, they are cut off, and I rationalize my next step.

Going to bed hungry is better than dining with him. But that won't be necessary as I'm an adult who can buy my own food and just see what I have in the cupboard. It's not about the food.

"Dad, I can no longer have dinner with you tonight," I assert calmly.

In that same instant, he ducks under the partitioned rope forming the line and bolts to his car, where he speeds off. He's gone.

I take my time walking to my apartment across the street, feeling rattled. Within ten minutes of slowing down my breathing and wiping my eyes, I see a text from my neighbor. He's inviting me up for dinner with his girlfriend and roommates, and I feel hopeful that love is available, abundant, and here.

2019, age 28, Santa Rosa, CA

It's my twin brother Thomas' wedding day and Ellie, his wife-to-be, who really wants us to get along and be close, has given me the option of a couple of poems to read. A beautiful tree-lined property in a woodsy area with a vineyard with ambient string lights and chairs in lines and tables with tablecloths. At golden hour, the couple are at the front of the space. I read the poem over and feel comfortable doing a live reading. I've been doing a lot more public speaking these days. My Auntie Jewel has thick dark brown curly hair and pale skin with freckles and got certified as a reverend online so she could officiate the wedding. If anyone could officiate my wedding, I'd want it to be her. But she says that after this one, she's probably done because it is a lot harder than she thought it would be. Jewel also got married a few years back and didn't invite me because she thought I would be busy, even though it was in San Francisco. I guess things have changed, and I accept this.

Ellie's desire to bond us with one another is sweet, though. She puts in effort to give me gifts and write me cards. I don't think she understands the depths of the disconnection, though. And how if Thomas isn't interested, this isn't going to work out as us becoming one big extended happy family. But one can dream, and her effort is seen and appreciated and I let her know that it's heart-warming to receive her level of sincerity and care.

We're all dressed up, and I don't know many people, but there are family members, including my grandpa from my dad's side who my dad says is mean, and part of me can see how he is meaner than my dad, and I'm glad we never got to know each other well. It's about making niceties, and while these days I typically spend time with my neighbors and friends, and enter events with excited anticipation of who I'll meet, this feels like an obligation. I'm less curious, but know how to placate the situation, and I do.

When it's time to read the poem aloud, I stand behind the podium and switch the mic closer to my lips, but not so close it will obstruct the sound. I'm in my element. These people don't know this side of me yet, some new, some up on the family gossip from years past. Now I'm someone channeling emotion into a poetry reading. Relating to the words and sharing it, connecting with the author in a way that fellow writers often like to. Anyway, I take a look at the paper I read through once before, breathe into a state of love, willing the love to radiate through the words I'm about to say, and speak the words aloud.

All I know About Love by Neil Gaiman. It ends,

" And because in the darkness you will reach out a hand, not knowing for certain if someone else is even there.

And your hands will meet, and then neither of you will ever need to be alone again.

And that's all I know about love."

People stand up to clap. I lightly smile and bow my head before sitting back down.

I can see how real and pure their love is. It's the stuff they deserve, and model so well, and I look forward to the day when that becomes my normal too. It's a loose sort of wanting. A kind of wanting that feels more like a nice-to- have than a necessity. I have friends, I've built a life, and sometimes I have these family things I am obligated to go to, so I oblige.

Any decent sister goes to their siblings' wedding even if they aren't on great terms. Even if we become estranged, I guess I'll always see people at weddings.

I stay until the wee hours of the morning since I'm carpooling with my cousin Sapphire. At one point a blackout drunk Karla, my sister who's two-and-a-half years younger, a middle child who resembles a younger version of my mom with her thick dark hair, starts air-guitaring and throws her body to the dance floor and has people roaring, especially my dad. He then gets out there and dances. It's the half of the year where he's sober, but Karla is inspiring him. I like that dynamic. Their full expression feeding each other. There's a sweetness in how some parents sometimes allow themselves to be influenced by their children.

2019, age 29, San Francisco, CA

I am in the final stretch, nearly a year of touring my workshop "Networking for Introverts" all around the US and abroad, being invited to share what I had learned at places I was surprised wanted to hear about my work: Harvard, a business community in Tokyo... and then, something that felt much bigger. I had submitted a few topics on September 12. One of which I felt certain they would choose based on my recent success with the niche, and one of which I didn't think they'd choose but felt core to my life: Shedding Labels.

I open up my email inbox on September 18, not even a week later.

"Good Morning Stephanie!

Thank you so much for this incredible submission. I am pleased to inform you that our organizer committee is very interested in your proposed topic and we would like to invite you to submit some additional documentation. We think your first topic about self-imposed labels would make a terrific addition to our program theme and we are very excited to see where you would like to take it..."

My mind is racing. My heart is heavy. How is it possible? I have been watching these videos on YouTube since I was a teenager, then behind-the-scenes at local TEDx events, and at this moment I am preparing to support my seventh TEDx, leading community, the event taking place in just a month. I was managing speakers in the green room at last year's event. I'm imagining how wild it would be to be in that position myself in 4.5 short months. I immediately reply asking about 2021 planning, since that topic is not one I am prepared to speak on in February 2020.

I rationalize: It's all the way in NYC and I'm about to fly there soon and going back in February is too soon. The venue had some previous videos that were not the best quality, so maybe this isn't the right venue for me. If it's meant to be, it can't pass me by.

But what I am really feeling was a rush to divulge what I have kept hidden for so long. I am just now getting established with this networking niche, claiming the title of confident introvert, and there's no way I can give a talk at SingSing, a prison, and not share that I've been where they are right now. Only a lot younger. Only for reasons I can't bear to speak out loud. It would be out of integrity to gloss over these facts of my life experience, so I won't do it and won't tell anyone about it, so they won't try to talk me out of backing out.

As the organizers excitedly ask to have a call to go over my speech outline and assure me it doesn't have to be perfect, I am riddled with shame and determined to instead embrace the label I have chosen, that people seem to resonate with and feels true for me, if only for a chapter or a few, and say, "I'm not ready yet. Thank you so much for the opportunity, but it has to happen later."

2019, age 29, Occidental, CA

"I know you probably don't read these." I hold a hand-written card from the passenger seat of his car.

My dad and I are stalled in front of the meditation center. He's dropping me off for my first silent *vipassana* meditation retreat. We are early, surrounded by trees and brush, and at a compound where people are still loading and unloading trucks with tables and chairs.

I just finished writing the first draft of my first book because I know I'd go crazy if I had to sit in silence for ten days without it finished. And there's another thing I feel I have to hit send on... feeling tears well up.

"I do," he whispers nervously, looking outside of the car window as though wishing to jump out of it.

"But you never respond," I challenge in a soft, matter-of-fact tone.

"I have read them. I just don't have anything to say.

You're very smart and your writing goes over my head."

"You haven't asked me to say it in simpler terms. And I have tried to phrase and rephrase my understanding of our relationship. And how we can move forward in a healthier way."

"You know, Stephanie, I like the way things are in my life. You just have to accept this is the way it is. Things aren't going to change." He shakes his head with an air of irritation.

Letting that sink in, I realize that this is the last letter. This is the last time I am doing this. There's nothing to come back to. I have to finally believe what I am hearing.

"I'm going to read this aloud right now so I know you hear it," I say softly, looking him square in the eyes.

"You don't have to do that." He looks away and contorts his body toward the car door.

"But I am going to." I look at the card in front of me, and see the words I've written, the tears fall and I say them, squeaking them through deep breaths, peering up at my dad, who chokes on sips of air as he gazes away stiffly.

"When I think of you, I imagine the character on the front of this card. Never mind that it's an elephant. The important thing is that he's sitting on a bench looking out at the water. A bird is on his hat and he doesn't seem to notice. I have a lot of pictures of you like that- standing off staring out at something when I am right behind you. I know it's not easy to talk about, but sometimes the hard conversations are worth it. I am not here to judge you or tell you that you're wrong. I am here to express my feelings with the goal that you will hear and acknowledge them... I've told you this before, but you were present growing up. For better or worse, you were there. This wasn't modeled for you, so it's a way you have begun to break the mold. Something that you and Mom never noticed — you talked about feeling left out of your own families, treated the worst, outside of the closeness, but that's exactly what happened when you were parenting me. It can be hard to see when you're so close to it, but it's been another lifetime over since all that happened, and maybe you can understand now. I can't be the only one trying. It feels so empty. I want to be myself and have it be okay, celebrated, and not just tolerated. Maybe you want or have wanted something similar." I gulp and am toward the end now.

"The energy it takes to try to connect with you and the family is energy that I could be spending helping people and contributing to the world. Our relationship is mediocre at best, and at other times unhealthy. We both deserve something better than mediocre and struggle. I am taking space from you as long as I need to. I will spend holidays with people who show they care about me in ways that I can understand."

I had said the same thing to my mom earlier that day, less formally. A boundary for them as well as myself. And I know I can trust my own word when it's given. He's still looking away, and I open the car door. With his eyes still averting mine, he reaches out for a half hug past the middle console, and I let him. My muscles limp, I exit the car, close the door too lightly. Then I tap on the trunk. He pulls the hatch to open it; I grab my bags, place them on the dirt road, and, in the same instant, watch him drive away.

2021, age 30, Rio Rancho, New Mexico

While cat sitting in New Mexico during the global pandemic, something shifts in me. There is not a lot going on in this city at this time in history, so I belatedly record the audiobook of my first book, careful to speak when meows are absent, and jog amongst the petroglyphs.

I create a document on my laptop and begin to pour out the names of all of the places I recall being checked into, all the educational, therapeutic, or punitive institutions during that time, well over a decade and a half ago now. Quite literally an entire lifetime over. I'm grateful that although life isn't perfect, and I still strive for certain relationship and career goals, I've come a lot further than a lot of people thought I could. Establishing friendships, some lasting chapters, others lasting what I believe can be a lifetime, or come in waves naturally ebbing and flowing. Being able to help people with their human connection skills and confidence and routinely doing work I love. Weekdays are spent virtually connecting with people on the other side of my zoom screen all across the US. I can see myself in them. Not just having experienced the pain and suffering of disconnection from their family, friends, partner, or self, but the glimmer in their eye as they speak, I listen, and like a highlighter, I repeat back the profound nature of what they just said. They say more, and I highlight another phrase or extrapolate their wisdom, and the best part is when they see it too without prompting. I'm not here to be someone's lifelong mentor, but to help shine a light on the value and inherent goodness that they themselves can let it grow and expand. I receive invitations to travel and speak at various conferences helping people authentically network and connect. It feels so validating that I get to teach the thing that didn't come naturally to me until I was in a new headspace and a new environment. Now, instead of simply visiting places I've always wanted to go, I just live there for a while, making friends in each new destination, continuing to share my deeper pondering or fun stories over WhatsApp, discovering more about the world and my place in it.

During a therapy session I recognize the deep empathy I feel for villains in stories, Maleficent, Cruella and so on, and how on some level it's because I see both myself and those who I felt have wronged me in the characters, not inherently bad, just misunderstood, or with good intentions that somewhere down the line were confused or lost as they traded in the desire for love for that of power. Which everyone knows on a deep level isn't really a suitable substitute.

Beyond what I do, it's how I feel. A sense of liberation that expands the more I acknowledge and accept the things that I cannot change from my past. Release the burden to assign or receive the blame in complex situations. A sense of agency and confidence to be selective in who I spend my time with, and the ways that I contribute to society, and trust myself even when it doesn't make logical sense to do so, or if there's fierce opposition. Paradoxically, this way of being has set the stage for me to invite more and more authentic connections into my sphere. What was once a dream.

And it's not necessarily a sense of pride that emerges, but an inner knowing, united with truth.

I know I was a hard kid to manage, defying authority, asking for more information or reasons if I didn't understand or agree with the way I was parented. Questioning everything, and that likely seeming critical and testing a new parent's patience and confidence. I don't regret it, but can empathize with an adult not knowing what to do with a kid like that. I'm also mindful to avoid painting a picture of my parents in a way I feel they painted me, as quite literally anything but good. We all have room to be better understood. I was less curious then, than I am now. Struggling to be heard, sharing how I felt in opposition to their words, none of us were receptive or submitting. I've learned to ask for consent before giving feedback since it feels so much better to dedicate time to deepen relationships where we share the desire to mutually understand one another.

Once the list of places is as full as my memory will allow, I treat it like a business development cold outreach campaign and get to work contacting each institution over email and by phone. Sometimes one of each for good measure. Phone is typically the best way to get the most immediate response across the board.

The conversations blur together.

"Hello, XYZ Institution," a monotone voice says expectantly, and without skipping a beat, I introduce myself. "Hi, I'm Stephanie Thoma, and I was a patient as a child, roughly 2001 to 2003 on and off. I'd like to request a copy of my records, please."

Many of the receptionists are responsive, wanting to help me unite with what records they still have, often suggesting, "Let me see how far our archives go back..."

The police records department voice on the other line are the most guarded, with "This is very unusual. I don't think anyone has ever asked us for this before. People typically only request the records of someone after they have died in a homicide, and it's been almost unheard of that a former juvenile detention inmate would want access."

I let her go through the motions of this discovery and bite my tongue before I can say, "There's a first time for everything," in an optimistic and sincere tone that would certainly be misconstrued.

Most people want to forget, I can assume from experience. A couple of institutions say that the records are not available since it's been more than ten years and they have been destroyed. The most significant paperwork I gain access to are the records of my childhood therapy appointments. A goldmine of a decade and a half of interviews, observations, speculations, and diagnoses.

I read through 296 of 400 pages on Friday, from ages four to fourteen, mostly hovering around age ten. It feels like investigating a cold case that has largely been dismissed as unsolvable. I want to try cracking the code.

Therapist notes. Police files. Hospital records. IEP statements. Me being referred to as needing to be "fixed" a "bad seed" as well as "lacking remorse" for "what I'd done," which was typically getting into a fight with a family member or refusing to be quiet when instructed to.

It's very clear my parents thought I had no ability to make friends and would probably never have an average life, let alone thrive socially because I was "constantly rejected by and irritating to peers," which I don't remember happening, but I do know I enjoyed chatting with adults more than having conversations with kids my own age. I also am noted by official tests to have below average confidence, but everybody agreed I exhibited leadership capabilities (mainly due to my ability to "debate" and "advocate" for myself). But I also showed symptoms of depression and resonance only with fictional characters I created or read about, that I don't remember today. "Guarded, hyper-vigilant with no tolerance for ambiguity and intellectualizing events." It's wild to me how observational it all is, with little regard for my emotional experience beyond what met the eye.

Moments of detachment as I read the words, a coping mechanism I had outgrown enough to catch when it happened, turned to being with myself. Placing my hand over my heart, deep breathing and feeling the wave of heaviness like a bag of cement migrate itself down my throat, through my chest, sometimes settling in my stomach resulting in a nauseating feeling. I would feel my body tense up and go limp. My mind, body, and soul were in this together, and I did my best to discard the desire to be graceful as the emotions surfaced and I listened to them with the patience of a parent who was determined to be there no matter what.

What I thought I had experienced was real. A melancholic relief, residing on the flip side of grief. Some of the practitioners even took note of slight things that validated the little hunches I had growing up. Like when a teacher liked me or didn't. I could read all of these adults without trying, as they were trying to read me.

When asked, I usually denied physical abuse, and everyone, both inside and outside of the family, seemed to deny it, too. But there's one mention of a time I said my mom scratched me and the report says they saw the scratch but I exaggerated how it happened and they believed it was an accident and I invited it by getting in her personal space when she was angry (wtf). I remember being afraid that if I told, I'd never get to go home again — it's so weird to me that there seemed to be a consensus: the home environment was labeled safe, and me as unsafe, instead of the other way around, or admitting it was just an unhealthy combination.

My Aunt Jewel lived in San Francisco and I'd see her at monthly board game nights at her apartment and she would come over to my parents' house around the holidays and birthdays, until she moved away, coincidentally, just before I moved there in my mid-20s. Jewel said on record that the household was "chaotic" and I "had my problems," but was ultimately the "scapegoat."

Routine checkboxes: Have you ever been physically abused, verbally abused, sexually abused?

I didn't know what it meant. The first time I answered these questions on paper was probably around the time I first learned to write cohesively, around six or seven. I asked my dad: "When you hit me, is it physical abuse?" His face reddened as it normally did before his gaze carried off distantly and his hands grabbed my entire body and threw it on the bed to rip down my pants and underwear and wail his palms onto me. Slap. Slap. Slap. Maybe he was being nice and holding back, I thought. It hurt, but maybe it could have hurt more, and I should have been grateful. What hurts the most is knowing that he wants to hurt me. "I'll give you something to cry about," he'd say, and I wondered why my reasons for crying already were not enough. Back to that moment, though, when I asked if this was abuse, he said with conviction: "Of course not! And you better not ever say you are or you'll never get to come back home again. It's just spanking. That is not abuse. My mom used to use a belt and whip us 'til we bled. You have it easy. You are NOT abused."

Around age seven, I thought it was so weird that as long as it was a spanking, it did not count as hitting, since hitting is abuse. But nobody questioned what we checked off. I still wondered. So, if he hit me other places than my butt, then it's all different? He had hit my head before- usually places that are covered by hair or clothing. But it's not about me being "right." I didn't want to be taken away. I didn't want to lie, so I never checked those boxes. Ages four to thirteen, always blank.

I knew better than to believe those strangers, stranger danger, when they said "this is between you and me, you can tell me..." I knew my parents had access to all my records — my dad once teased me about how "mean" I made him out to be. I had no privacy, and I didn't want to lie, so it's all blank.

Confirmed: in 2003, my dad requested copies of all the files I have now requested in 2021. ALL the notes of my mom feeling like my dad criticizes her weight, doesn't support her, or any time I vaguely called him "mean," he has had all of my private records for his personal use for eighteen years. As far as I know, my mom does not have a copy and probably doesn't know he has them. I wonder if he knew starting in 2008 when I became an adult, he would lose access. I hope that I am still protected by the law against whatever his intention was for having his own copy.

When questioned, "Do you think there's hope for Stephanie?" that same year, 2003, when I was twelve, my dad said, "Absolutely not, she's a lost cause, hopeless." And my mom said, "I'd like to think there's always hope."

Update: Judge says she will mail my records this month.

The judge has asked for a completed JV-5740 form after a ten-minute call after receiving the request to unseal and share the record. The judge showed concern around word choices such as "learning what accusations were," saying "You can't publish this if we share it with you." The judge made it clear that the request is unusual and that if she doesn't find the reason compelling, she will dismiss the request to retrieve juvenile records. She says looking into the full reports and mental health records will also determine her decision.

2021, age 30, Petaluma, CA

Karla didn't invite me to be in her wedding party of bridesmaids. While her closest friends and select family members were receiving letters inviting them to be a part of it, I at least got the decency of a written card signaling my exclusion. It caused a fuss with my mom and Cassie. "She's your sister," they said to her.

But, I said something different. "Thank you for being true to yourself." This is what I think, ego aside. But when I feel into it, I can't help but notice this was an opportunity to include me that was not taken. It could have been a moment of reconciliation, allowing me to celebrate one of her biggest days, and support her like the big sister I always wanted to be for her, but I won't fight it. Her mind is made up. My letter was letting me know she didn't want me to be in it since "we're not close." And it's true, but the sting is there, nonetheless. We're not and now we will not be. Why fight reality unless both people want to make some radical change? The best example I feel I can lead with as a big sister is to caretake my own emotions, and honor her for doing in essence what I have chosen to do — intentionally create space for those who 'get it,' and with grace, provide space from those who year after year, chronically don't.

I look on the bright side of not having to spend all the time and money that is inevitable when you're in a wedding party; however, I also yearn to have women in my life close enough that I would gladly take it all on. The self-soothing is falling a bit flat at times as the truth of the potential of this relationship that is 'supposed' to be close seeps in, and I strive to accept what comes and goes, hand on my heart, breathing, sometimes wailing.

This doesn't stop me from attending her bridal shower. After all, she invited me, and if I'm going to attend the wedding as a guest in the crowd instead of a bridesmaid up there alongside her, this is a good litmus test.

I enter the party and see her laughing and passing mini bottles of champagne around, hugging every one of the 2 dozen or so guests. She's the queen of the party, curvy and taking up space in stature and personality in her feminine floral dress. I know better than to interrupt her conversations and situate myself near the cupcakes until she comes over to give me the kind of hug where your chests are held apart so they don't touch and your fingertips lightly tap the other person's upper back in the moment you slightly hunch toward each other. She seems so happy. She's definitely the most Pinterest-friendly celebration family member, with name tags and assorted pastel sharpies when you walk in, upscale barnyard chic scented candles lit and color coordinated Easter-egg colored wedding themed decorations lining her newly renovated kitchen.

I see her friends and smile with a soft "Hello" and there's a vibe. They glance at me with the types of smiles that are absent from the eyes—lips only, forcefully lifting then dropping as quickly as their hands gesture to say "Hello" out of politeness. It feels like a statement to be here. In a place where I am so clearly not wanted, tolerated, but it isn't about me, so I can handle it.

After about twenty minutes of being a fly on the wall, observing the people Karla has come to treasure both in friendship and family, she rallies everyone to get together. A few rows of people. All women, my mom, our mutual sister, all her friends from work and school, her bridal party, of course.

She looks at me and asks, "Can you take the picture?"

To which I say without thinking, "Yes," and immediately stifle the intense jabbing emotion in my heart that's taken hold.

I take the picture and ask everyone to smile, and take a few more for good measure. Then I return her camera to her.

She gregariously exclaims, "Thank you!" Either oblivious or not connected to what just occurred.

At the same moment, I feel my tear ducts swelling and remember, this isn't about me, and also recognize, I did a good deed, she now has a photo with everyone she cares about at this party, and I walk out the door.

I don't have a car. This is what San Francisco life does to you since everything is so walkable until you leave the city. I start walking and let the tears fall. Private streets in Petaluma on a warm afternoon. No people around, just me, in the heat, walking until I find a place that looks private enough to sit down on the curb and let the tears fall as I continue to muffle the sound in case anyone walks by.

I stay there for twenty minutes, considering that I might get the courage to go back, but intuit that when I re-enter those doors, the waterworks will start, and it's not the kind of entrance I care to make. It's about her special day. I call my dad and can barely get the words out... "I need... to go home," I sob.

And he doesn't ask why. "Where are you?"

I list the cross streets, and within fifteen minutes, he's there.

I continue to cry when I get in the car and he doesn't say anything.

Cassie texts me asking where I am, and I say *I left*.

She says, *I wish you stayed.* :) Dad understands, which I have mixed feelings about. I'm sure he understands because of the impact he had on this established dynamic growing up, vilifying and othering me. The other children were taught to take sides: validate your parents and invalidate your sister, or you're just as bad as her. They were dependent on parents for everything, so what do you think they'd choose? It's like it was set up to turn out this way with us, and it would take an amount of defiance to break that I haven't seen in anyone in the immediate family but myself or my dad.

I write Karla a short letter commending her authenticity and sharing how I will honor mine. I do not attend her wedding the following year, and decline a friend's wedding invitation for the exact same day as hers, being overwrought with emotions, not wanting to choose a friend over a sister. Instead, I spend that day in a brand new apartment in an obscure corner of Philadelphia, absolutely alone. I write music, poetry, and journal between client calls, creating YouTube content and staying connected with my pre-COVID community through my weekly email newsletter, instead. This is during my digital nomad chapter, and I have been good about continuing to take therapy calls as something constant while everything changes. I read a poem aloud to my therapist and she says, "That sounds like it could be a song." When the call ends, the melody flows through my ears and before I can forget it, I record it. I call it Villainize.

2021, age 31, New York, NY

Life is largely on hold, and I'm spending time in a new city around the holidays. Memories seep in, and random items end up in my grocery cart. Because when I have pistachio ice cream,

I think of Dad. I don't even like it much. It's a flavor I know he always liked, and probably still does. And whenever I have a Milano cookie, although I don't even like those either, it's like we're watching bad reality tv dating shows like elimi-date until the wee hours. Mom and me. I buy these things because they feel familiar and there's a comfort. Imagining how they'd feel if they knew. That I'm more like them than they think. In some ways I choose, others I don't.

I can light up a room, help others feel welcome and comfortable and laugh with gusto like my mom. But we also sometimes stay home for days on end in our robes feeling not so great.

I can put my head down and complete whatever work I am committed to, whether I feel like it or not, and maintain a fitness routine, like my dad. But we also can be stubborn in a way that people don't always like my dad.

It's bittersweet, how these sweets remind me of the good times. I try my best to keep those memories more top-of- mind, even when it's hard.

2023, age 32, Novato, CA

Mom texts to come up into the house to get some bonds my late grandma left for me. Dad will explain them to me. I walk into the two-story house and use the restroom to the immediate right. The one that I'd always used is now spruced up with candles and lotions for guests, and a seashell theme I imagine as commemorating me, my camp name was Shelley since I have always loved seashells so much. The little details like this keeping the relationship alive someone staying in that room may not be privy to.

    I walk out, nobody else in the house, and linger in the remodeled kitchen, still with a barnyard vibe, but with more natural wood and black touches with dried lavender. It feels elevated. Pictures of the kids hang up on that space and little ones of me. My college graduation photo rests on the mantle, and I feel a jolt of grief looking at my smiling face from a decade ago, graduating from college on Father's Day. I can understand that seeing my face, from a time when I was willing to do anything to make this work, could be daunting. I could leave now and not see him, but instead, I go to the fridge and pour myself a glass of cold pressed carrot juice I can tell is from Costco and chug it. Then I grab a Starbucks mug and patiently wait as the contents of the k-cup drips into it, decaf coffee, noting in real time the sabotage of consuming even a trace amount of caffeine at a time like this, but I no longer care. Maybe I'm not welcome to these things as their estranged daughter. Maybe I am. Goodness knows I'm not asking permission and I feel a bit guilty and silly for it. I linger a moment longer, placing the dishes in the dishwasher that may not go undetected in a nearly empty-nested home with Tyler who's in his early 20s, nearly a decade younger than me, the last of their children still living here, before walking back down to where I parked the car, sitting in the driver's seat in nervous anticipation. And then they pull up, my mom's big green Lexus at the top of the hill, as the car I'm in is in the side parking place. I get out of the car.

    I see him through the barren winter tree branches. He is atop the hill, and I'm below, camouflaged in a way, wearing all black. He looks older than when I last saw him in 2020. My heart races as I walk up the steps leading me to that familiar house on the hill, feeling like I know him, but over the years, he's become mythologized — the man from the story I wrote.

My mom, who is wearing her usual robe, meets me as I'm still walking up the steps and tells me she lost seventy pounds from a gastric sleeve, but I can't really tell because, well, the robe. She and I both cry with our faces on each other's shoulders. Dad can probably hear as he's in earshot.

"I want you to know that I love you, and I always will. I can't go back in time, but we can move forward," she pleads.

"I love you too, and we are doing our best. I'm not going to be the type of kid that spends holidays here. As the years go by, we'll find what works," I offer.

We hug for the first time in nearly one thousand days. The kind of hug that warms me like cookies my mom never used to bake. There's a distinct quality in a mom hug. And if I retreat into it, I almost feel like it's all okay, and nothing else needs to matter right now. The tears stream with the contrast of how close I wish we could be, and even though we are physically close right now, once we pull apart, I know that a hug can be healing. It isn't everything, but what if I let it be? What if we don't try to talk it out anymore, no phone calls or letters, just a familiar, longing, knowing hug that only your mother can give you? She goes back up the steps and inside the house.

I inch closer up the hill as in slow motion, each wooden step inserted into the raw earth, some jiggling with a simple step, and I see my dad averting his eyes. His energy is focused on me, and I know it. He keeps his distance, at least a yard, and calls out information about stocks. When I mentioned I'd be coming back to get the things I left in the shed, I didn't anticipate missing items, others mangled with rat bites. A sense of grief and then detachment at my 'investment pieces' that exemplified my time in downtown San Francisco in my twenties are all tattered or no longer there.

As I was saying, he looks older than he did before. His gray hair has turned to white, and I realize he's nearly entered his seventies since I last saw him.

Eye contact averted, three feet away, he rambles, "Did you know that there are two types of bonds that you have... I told your grandma Laverne to get the other ones... I told her to go with more II bonds but she got half EEs. You can just cash them now since they won't appreciate much more, and the cash value is better off in a bank."

It's his typical monologue and in a window of silence I ask, "Can you help me find some missing things? My coats... they are completely missing except for one."

Meanwhile, Mom has gotten into her car, and seems she is waiting for somebody, stalling. She begins to take pictures from her car window of us in the garage like a paparazzo.

"Dad, she is taking pictures of us," I sigh as I shake my head and note her infatuation with family pictures, which leaves me feeling without words, but not surprised. Yes, even if we are three yards apart, she wants to document this moment.

"Jean," Dad scoffs.

She rolls down the window and, in a baby voice, says, "What?" and stops taking pictures.

Dad and I walk to the barn area, and he finds a bag. It's crusted with a coat of dust and filled with clothes he said he would donate years ago. No sign of a significant portion of my things and I feel disappointed yet not surprised.

"I don't know what to tell ya," Dad says and continues telling me about bonds as

Mom texts me, *Come to Starbucks with me for coffee!*

Thanks, but I'm not a big coffee person, I text back, recalling the one cup that is enough for the day.

Mom has driven off to Starbucks with Tyler and Dad is talking about stocks as I nod only occasionally. I stand there and wonder if he will try to hug me and if I'm open to it, and I decide that I am. He finishes talking, we look at each other, and there's a pause.

"I should get going," I say with tears in my eyes. "Take it easy," he says in a forced, casual tone.

As I get back into my car, I know I have to be the one. I have to say it. I draft a text on my phone. *Dad, can you please hug me before I go?* And I sob harder at the vulnerability of pressing send while sitting in the car with a purse full of savings bonds intended to last me my whole life.

"I don't know how you're doing financially, but this can't hurt," he had said as he handed them off.

We don't owe each other anything, and it's apparent this is another act of goodwill, of human decency, me getting my things, and him passing the bonds off, then there's nothing left to keep me here — no money or things. And oh, how I wish there was more than that. The realization of grief that cannot be denied takes over, weighing heavily in my chest like an anchor that instinctively wants to root itself into the soil, as I muster all the strength I have to hold it steady. I don't believe that anyone is inherently toxic, but as a combination, we are toxic to each other. It's like we need to be 'dead to one another' to grieve how we wish it was, to have a chance at, maybe someday, reuniting and being able to accept a more surface-level and casual dynamic that once felt unacceptable, at least to me.

Sometimes, being "the bigger person," you crumble a little. I can see the ways we're the same and the ways we're different. I know he'd be too proud to show affection if he wasn't certain it'd be reciprocated, whereas in this moment I'm just going with what I feel, with intention. To have a chance to be met, not to inspire new hope, but to solidify a way of being. When people are in front of me, I'll consider their feelings, and even if I need to speak through my tears, with as much love as I can muster, I'll speak my own. I know what I want in life, more or less. What I have to give. I'll stop trying to dictate how I get it. This moment is like peeking through a door before you close it.

He knocks on my window, and I open the door.

"The answer is yes!" he says as though he's on a dating game show, and it's so very him, half joking, half serious. He walks over to me with limp arms, and his posture is stiff, giving the type of hug someone gives when they are out of practice, maintaining a sense of hovering so that you don't actually make contact.

I don't have the energy to correct the hug, feeling spent having initiated it. I cry harder.

He tenses up, loosens his grasp further, and I hear him say, with a scoff, "You're going to be all right. You're going to be alright." He says the words over and over again, and I'm not sure if he's trying to convince himself or me.

It reminds me of when I saw Grandma Judith so many years ago when I was in the hospital. "Take care of yourself," she'd say repeatedly.

I wanted so badly for someone to want to take care of me when I was a tween.

I choke on any words I could have said, knowing that it has already been spoken. It hurts like this because I care. It hurts like this because, as my friend, who happens to be a therapist, has said, we're "chronically misattuned."

Dad's voice trails off, repeating that phrase "you're going to be alright..."

I sit back in my car and say, "I love you." He says, "I love you too."

And I drive away.

I'm learning to redirect the love I had been trying to give others who cannot receive it inward instead. This instance wasn't as much about trying to get bread from a hardware store as much as proclaiming *I want bread* in front of the hardware store before leaving it, if only for the sake of expression and clarity instead of stifling what was real for me. And now, to fill up my own cup for a time, if not always, and share the bulk of what I cultivate with those who can possibly receive it. No matter how selfish those who believe they should have it directed toward them may feel it is, I get to choose.

There's an acceptance that if this is it, this is it, while being open to something shifting as things can while space exists between them. This is letting go.

I'm learning I've been in shame-based relationships that demanded perfection or conforming to personality standards until I decided to replace my own self-judgment with the curiosity I so often look at others with.

Asking internally, "Can I love the parts of myself that people once outcasted?"

"Can I show those pieces to others, not for the sake of validation, but freedom?"

"Can I choose curiosity over shame and lead my life from that place?"

"What do I need to do to forgive myself and those involved in the situations that hurt my heart?"

I have had this conversation with myself before, but it is getting deeper now.

2. FIRST LOVE

2006-2011

"Hear her, redeem her."

- "Villainize" by Stephanie Thoma

2006, age 15, Novato, CA

My Aunt Jewel told me that my parents' problems didn't go away when they sent me away. She and I both knew I wasn't the cause of their problems, and now they finally realize that too. Mom and Dad tell me how they *really feel* about the other, as though they want my advice now. Probably because I've had more therapy than both of them combined. I just ask, "Have you told them that? It's not appropriate to tell me this. Tell them that, instead."

Talking with my new therapist, Hannah, is fun. She's in her mid-20s with large expressive light blue eyes and straight light blonde hair in a side part with a clip and slim fitted business casual clothing. She usually compliments me and tells me I'm deep. I can brag to her and she is even happier than I am. "I won the 5k race around the track. I even beat all the guys," I share matter-of-factly after the weekly race we have in P.E. (physical education).

She even encourages me to try out for the local cross- country team. "They need you," she says, "they'll be better with you. Just try it."

So, the next day at school, I ask my gym teacher if I can try out for the cross-country team. "It's not cross-country season, it's the middle of track season, but you can train with them over the summer and start in the fall." I decide to connect with the team and join their summer training.

It is the summer of 2006 that I have places to go and a group of people to see. My new cross-country friends and I run together, spend hours talking as we ride to and from beautiful scenic trails, and share meals. They like to study like me and I'm impressed most of them get nearly perfect grades as well. It's a feeling of easy connection where I can relax into the endorphins from running and the easy-going, conscientious nature we all seem to share when we're together.

— —

They say they are taking me out for my birthday. It's a big one. Sweet sixteen. Last year was different, and now I'm home "for good." I don't want to spend my special day with them, but this is what you do when you're not sick. When you are a functioning member of society. You prioritize family. I ask to celebrate another day; my mom defers to my dad. They say that we are celebrating the same day as my twin. But what about where I want to go? I don't like Chinese food that much, and it's Thomas' favorite. I prefer foods like fresh spinach and grilled salmon.

"If you want to go with us, you can, but don't be difficult." Dad cautions firmly.

"How am I being difficult by wanting to celebrate my birthday with the people and food I want?" I correct.

"Ungrateful. The world doesn't revolve around you. Are you coming or not?" Dad asks bluntly.

"Yes," I say before going into my room to cry.

They don't care what I like or want. I think of it as a free meal, but then doesn't that make me selfish? I cannot force myself to feel love and care. The guilt is paralyzing. To know that I must act in ways that cause me grief. Guilt for not doing what is expected, or grief for my true self and desires. Who do I choose? What should I do? I've always wanted to choose myself, but my parents and most other people I know say that's not right. It feels bad either way. I am so confused. They'll be mad if I don't go, and if I do, everything will be fine. *Just* fine.

Dad says we're leaving at 5:45pm for a 6:30pm reservation. It takes ten or maybe fifteen minutes to drive there. I get a sick feeling in my stomach.

He yells for me, "Come out now!" then the door slams and the car horn honks.

I am writing and want to continue. I don't move from my room. Paralyzed. Why would I go closer to the chaos? The noise? The people who care more about the idea of celebrating me, for the sake of a picture with mouth-only smiling? For the way it looks instead of how it feels. I stay seated on that brown carpet, realizing this game that I have re-entered. Every place I've been has been a game and I know all the rules, but why can't I just play by them? Follow the script? It would be a selfless thing to do. But today, on my birthday, I choose myself and I breathe deeply. Sitting still. Breathing still. Will they leave without me? I'm not rushing. I'm not stalling. I'm contemplating this and removing the expectation from myself without haste. And then I begin to walk outside. It's quiet. I'm curious.

They are gone.

I'm not even surprised. It feels like a rite of passage, to be left behind. A metaphor of the feeling that's always been there. But this time, I put my comfort first instead of springing into action that felt wrong anyway. I feel a swirl of melancholy and peace. Perhaps this time, being alone can be the very best thing.

2006, age 16, Novato, CA

We're at Christmas dinner and Dad's drunk again. He says he doesn't have a problem, because he is only drinking half of the year, not the other. Or because he takes a day per week off. Or it's only on holidays. But I think it's still a problem even if you control it sometimes. How about controlling it all the time? Mom says he's "better when he's drinking," and it makes me sad. People think he's better when he's not like himself. I relate.

He's fifty-three at the dinner table this Christmas.

Anyway, there's silence after dinner, and Dad starts rambling. "When I'm old, Karla, you're going to help me." He points directly at her (she's thirteen). "Thomas, you're going to help me when I'm old." Then, "Cassie, you're going to help me when I'm old," (she's eleven). Tyler is six and not at the table. "Stephanie, you are *not* going to help me when I'm old."

I look away. I don't know the answer to this question and it's not even a question... what kind of help would he want? "Why not, Dad?" I ask.

"You're just not going to help me. You can mark my words. You'll be the only one. You are not going to help me."

Shortly after, he stumbles up the stairs and goes to sleep. My understanding is he wanted to have a lot of kids as a sort of insurance policy, in case something like this happened. In case he had a daughter like me, but I'm "better" now, right? Maybe not totally "fixed" by their standards, but nobody can say I'm not *better*. People continue having conversations and I'm stuck on that sentence. Is it that he thinks I won't offer, or that he'll know better than to ask?

2007, age 16, Novato, CA

After almost two book-end summers, one year together as a team, it's clear: the cross-country team are "my people." We spend weekends making bonfires and s'mores, jogging along trails and ghost riding the whip, which is this fad where you'd have the car in neutral with nobody in the driver's seat as you are dancing with the door open aside it as it coasts. Some of our parents think we drink, but nope, we actually don't. It's just so fun to be with them.

One day we are at the beach and the summer of 2007 is coming to a close. Many of my senior friends have graduated and I'll be the senior in just a week or so. I bring chocolate cupcakes made with nothing but cake mix and Dr. Pepper. I accidentally spill them into the sand when I arrive, and they're eaten, anyway. They're not mad that I dropped them at all. And one of them brought a friend. His name is Benjamin, and he has a bowl haircut and somehow is always sitting near me or looking at me. I wonder why, but not too much. It feels good to talk with him. He's very attentive and repeats back things I say and his eyes are lit up with a soft smile.

— —

I ask a friend of ours why he does so much for me, as he grabs my jacket I'd left in his car one day as we're grabbing burritos for lunch.

"Just let him do it," he says. "He knows you can do it yourself, but he's doing it because he really wants to."

And I let that sink in.

2007, age 17, Novato, CA

When the summer is over, most of the crew is off to college. I'm a senior this year, promoted to team captain. One day soon after the school year starts, Kelsie hand-delivers me a hand-written letter.

"Dear Stephanie,

I didn't say everything I wanted to say to you the other night, and I didn't want to wait to tell you. I'm falling for you as hard as Kelsie fell that one night ☺

So, we agree the distance thing is an issue. You didn't seem interested in such a thing and I completely understand. Let me know if you change your mind because I'd be down for trying my best to make it work — you're most definitely worth it.

Well, I never thought I'd meet someone so wonderful. I feel really lucky to know the one and only you.

Much love, Benjamin"

I read it and feel a surge of energy course through my entire body and an uneasy, queasy sensation. It's from Benjamin.

I can't explain it, but I feel repulsed. Is he falling in love with me? But he doesn't know me. Everything is so nice and I feel it must be fake. I don't know how I feel about him. It's a nice feeling, but these feelings of his are pretty darn strong. Why is he telling me this? What does he hope to gain? A part of me feels sick and another part of me kind of likes it.

Nobody's ever written me a letter like that. I never asked for it. I put the letter away and let things settle.

I reply over AOL messenger when he asks if I received his letter.

"Yup, I got your note — sry for not getting in touch sooner, but I've been thinking about it... something tells me starting a relationship 'long distance style' just wouldn't work. Usually, people who've been dating for over a year or so and then go off to college do that sort of thing. I really want you to be able to experience your first year at college knowing that your options are wide open. It wouldn't be fair to either of us because, in all honesty, we don't know each other all that well beyond superficial things. There's a lot more to me than liking "The Hush Sound," and more to you than playing the tenor sax.

Of course I like you, and you like me — which is cool because it's rare that works out that way, but starting out with a computer being the only thing to keep us together. hmm...I'm sort of rambling at this point, and I'm sure I've restated reasons why we should preserve the friendship for now, but I just want to let you know all the factors I've considered."

2008, age 17, Novato, CA

"You have really good sound. But can you try that one part again?" Benjamin asks.

Benjamin has olive skin, extra tanned from his time in sunny Los Angeles and being half Puerto Rican. He just finished his freshman year at a private school there and we have been in touch periodically and I think we saw one another during Winter Break. He has a thin, lanky build, and medium length (and growing) shaggy, wispy dark hair. I am sitting in his room and recording a song for my high school jazz choir class final.

I never learned how to read music, but I'm lucky to have what Benjamin calls "perfect pitch," so I memorized in real time during tryouts and passed the sight reading. I am sitting cross-legged on the floor of his childhood bedroom, next to a twin bed with plaid bedding and his keyboard. I'm holding the mic he has for me, as he is watching lines of audio peter in and out with my words.

The lyrics are heavy, but we add a fun jingle at the end.

"Thank you, everyone, for coming... it's been a blast." I say in a giggly tone.

"Hey ya'll, I'm Ben!" Benjamin chimes in while playing a sing-songy piano jingle. "That was pretty fun, wasn't it?" he asks.

Without skipping a beat, I laugh heartily. "Yeah!" and the laughter trails off along with the jingle, and that's a wrap.

I play it for my class that same month and recognize it's so different from how they perceive me. Laughter and airiness. Contrasted by dark lyrics, they are undoubtedly making it mean something it's not. A light and darkness that gives depth to the usual monochrome gray vibe I imagine I am at best, blending in, not making a fuss, and getting my school work done unnoticed. But Benjamin sees me in color.

— —

I won a scholarship in high school, which kind of surprised me. It was for the most volunteer hours and I shared the honor with a male classmate. Although the guy doubled the suggested one hundred hours, I tripled it. The school decided we each deserved the award and should split it into $250 each instead of $500 for one of us. I notice this with a sense of amused detachment. I also consider that about one hundred hours was court mandated even though I would have done it anyway, but we were *even*, I suppose, since something tells me he didn't have a court mandate for *any* of his hours. There's something about volunteering that really got me: I could help kids have fun, be that person who understands them, and when you do a great job, especially beyond mediocre, sometimes you get gratitude. But most of the time you don't, and that is okay.

One of my favorite times working with kids is as a camp counselor for a summer and nature camp, leading a group of girls throughout the day and sometimes over the course of a week. Babysitting is the best, because I can do what I love and get paid for it at the same time. Sometimes the kid I care for runs the show or is a little sassy, and I don't care. If they want to play a game, we will play that game. If they want me to bark like a dog, you bet I will happily oblige. If they argue with a boundary that their parents hadn't set in stone, like what to eat or not eat for dinner, I reflect back their desires, and reach a compromise with them to show their thoughts and feelings not only matter, but expressing them and advocating for themselves can evoke real change. As long as they get to experience their power in a healthy way, it is second-hand vindication.

Over my high school years, I remember feeling a sense of apathy, an aversion to success, or being recognized. During my senior year, I tried out for and was accepted into jazz choir, and earned a solo that was cut before we were about to perform. People expressed their condolences that I would never have the experience of singing a solo in choir in high school. I rationalized that I can sing solo whenever I want to.

I've learned not to do things for other people's reactions, since they are often unpredictable.

I was ready to be a first-generation college student. My friend group that bred valedictorians and salutatorians made an impression on me. It was normal and a non-negotiable to go to college after high school, whereas in my family it was a nice-to-have/maybe. I was initially accepted into CSU Channel Islands to be among their first graduating class. The campus was a restored mental asylum where, apparently one day, everyone on the ward was taken into a bus and dropped off in San Francisco. I found the prospect of being in a reformed mental institution darkly comedic, and also empowering if you count that it would be of my own accord, bettering myself for my future life impact, and my goal of living in San Francisco one day. The thing is, I am not great at math (except statistics and some geometry), and when my final grade came out as a D+ where I had needed a solid C to maintain the acceptance, it was revoked. I ended up enrolling in a community college for the first two years before transferring to another (better) school, University of California, Santa Barbara. That also meant more time at 'home' to save money. Keeping my future self in mind, I accepted the charity. It's more socially appropriate when you're an early-twenty-something, anyway. I got a job during the day in Sausalito and took night classes in Santa Rosa, clocking 100 miles per day in my car. As I grew my base of knowledge and funds, I was hardly home, and it worked out for this time overall. I wanted to be in a place where, once I left, I'd never have to come back.

— —

Benjamin invites me on a first date at his parents' house during the summer before he heads off to college again. Apparently, he paid for their dinner out so he could have the house, which is a sweet gesture for everyone involved. He says he wants to "take me in" instead of out and while in any other situation going on a first date to someone's house would be creepy, I've been to his house so many times before, so it feels okay. He has cooked us grilled salmon with a confit in the middle, grilled vegetables, and couscous. I've never had that last one before. We share in-depth conversation as he serves food onto my plate. It's so nice. After dinner, he drives me home, and while it didn't feel terribly romantic, it felt good. I liked it. A lot, actually.

One summer evening, Benjamin comes through the side entrance of my room. It's late at night and it feels like those scenes in Clarissa Explains It All, although he doesn't need to use a ladder. He's come over before, and we just talk, but this time I'm in a new nightgown, and it's white and light blue with eyelet lace. It's a soft cotton with thin adjustable straps that looks like something a nice Southern girl from the prairie would wear. Something my mom got me because she said it looked sweet. I put a bra on underneath it, then take it off moments before he arrives and I don't know why, it just feels right. He comes over, and now I know why I didn't wear a bra.

2008, age 18, Novato, CA

It was a sort of vow I'd made myself early on.

With all the chaos and labels that swirled around my head, at least I hadn't gotten involved with any boys. At least I was "good" and "pure" in those ways.

So, no matter what anyone says about the way I naturally showed up, I'm good.

Here's something nobody is even telling me not to do, that I just-so-happen to not be doing.

Ultimate empowerment, right?

It isn't until my first boyfriend that I even reconsider it.

We are having a frank discussion on the topic of progressing our relationship that I still have not allowed him to put a label on.

I share the promise I made to myself.

I don't mention this to him, but my parents don't care if I have sex. They let my twin brother's girlfriend sleepover all the time, let them rent out hotel rooms. You could even say they are "sex positive" and I don't recall them really saying anything bad about the act. It's like a sort of rebellion that I'd have a hangup on something they cared so little about.

The fear is very real...of no longer having anything to make myself "pure" or "good."

Not because my parents ever said that to me. It's something I decided for myself.

Even though they don't care what I do sexually and probably think I've already done it, there is a pride in knowing I haven't. But now that I'm considering it, my self- prescribed "goodness"...

it's hanging on by a thread.

— —

We get in the habit of going into the shed at night when we are both in our hometown during summer and winter breaks. Loaded with dozens of porcelain dolls, knick-knacks, and a fold-out couch. He meticulously clears the floor of junk, turns on the rusty light bulb dangling above us, lays a clean quilted blanket down to make out in private.No more worrying that anyone will walk into the kitchen, visible from the living room to get water, which somehow happens often.

We play music to set the mood and detract from the odd ambiance of clowns and dust and trinket animal figurines and old movie posters. Lil Wayne's "Lollipop" comes on. This song is simply inspiring me. And then he says it's my turn.

"So, you should know something... that I'm on my period. You can still touch me, right? I'm okay with you doing it, but I just don't want you to find me disgusting," I express.

"I could never find you disgusting," he says with steady eye contact, and I feel safe. "Besides, it may ease your cramps." I lie back with a light feeling in my heart.

— —

We write letters to one another and lengthy emails every three days. I think he times them that way. Sometimes we'll carve out eight hours to video chat. I wish he was nearer, but this is all we can do for now while we are each going to college in different cities. Just to make it work. I know he wants me to be his girlfriend and as time goes by, I get more comfortable with the idea.

— —

2009, age 18, Novato, CA

One day Benjamin calls me. "Hey want to go to Mardi Gras? We can visit my brother there and stay with him. I can get our tickets, what do you think?"

Well, I'd never thought of going there before, but it would be interesting. I have only been out-of-state that one time, and then on the Germany trip I booked for myself. Wouldn't it be cool to see somewhere new? "You know, I think I should be free. Do you know the sleeping situation?" I ask, as though we haven't already slept in the same bed before. Is this how he wants to have sex for the first time? Do I want that? I wonder.

"I'm not sure...I can check. The prices are going up though, so should I get them?"

Classic sales tactic, but I do want to go, actually.

"Sure, thanks Benjamin. I think it will be a lot of fun to explore with you."

Hours pass and I fantasize about the trip. What an amazing experience! How nice of him. What will it be like to be in New Orleans? And I get another call.

"Hey what's up?" I ask, and there's a pause.

"Hey, so I can't get your ticket anymore. I'm sorry." "What changed?" I ask, feeling frazzled.

"I just can't. But if you want to get yours, you can. It's two hundred forty dollars."

"I don't have that kind of money, Benjamin. Then I guess I can't go?"

"I guess not. Thanks for understanding." "Of course, good bye."

And as the phone hangs up, I feel my eyes welling with tears and I'm sobbing, body shaking sobs. I call my Aunt Jewel to talk through what is happening. I come to some realizations.

"You have to tell Benjamin, Steph."

"Oh my god, no. It's too personal," I whisper.

"Steph, you gotta. I know it won't be easy, but if you don't, you're robbing him of the opportunity to make it right. You can do this."

And I know it's true. With a deep breath, my body still trembling, I call him, and he answers. "Hey... so... I'm having a hard time," I utter, barely catching my breath.

"Is everything okay? Have you been crying? What happened?" he asks, concerned.

"I don't think I can say it. You'll judge me or think it's not a big deal." My breathing grows heavier.

"You can trust me. You can tell me. I can wait until you're ready."

"Okay... so... when I was little... maybe six or seven... my dad would always tell me he was going to take me to Germany for my 14th birthday. Every year since I can remember, I was looking forward to it. Then the year came, when I was fourteen.

He corrected it was actually always going to happen when I turned fifteen.

Then I was fifteen, he said it was actually sixteen.

Then, several months before my sixteenth birthday to give us enough time to plan, I reminded him, and he told me that yes, he had said he would take me when I was sixteen, but it was only if I was good. And I had been bad, and I no longer deserved it. He didn't take me. I felt so heartbroken. And you know, I saved up and took myself to Germany last year for my 18th birthday, but still, this makes me feel just like that did. Getting my hopes up, feeling excited and then it disappears. I feel so let down and I haven't stopped crying since we got off our call hours ago."

"Stephanie, I don't want to be someone who lets you down. Don't tell my mom, but I'll get you the ticket. You can count on me. But you have to promise to never tell my mom."

"I promise. I have no reason to share that with her." I feel soothed and calm and... elated.

I call Auntie Jewel and she says, "Wow, what a guy. I like him. He has character. He's true to his word. Well, my sweets, have fun in New Orleans!"

A letter before the trip:

"Dear Stephanie,

Your package was an incredibly sweet surprise!!

That was really thoughtful of you :). Thanks for the chocolate — I just ate 3 pieces and they were all satisfyingly yummy mhmm.

I would love to have a V-day with you when I come home :) I like this idea. It could be even more special than the 14th because it would be just about us — a holiday to call our own. I look forward to it very much. Spending time with you is always awesome and special to me.

You are an amazingly sweet girl and I feel really blessed that you are a part of my life. I want you to know that you are always on my mind and that I care about you so sooo much. It won't be long before we get to see each other again (I am smiling as I wrote this).

Love, Benjamin"

Someone who finally "gets" me. Someone I can share my most random thoughts with, be silly with and serious with. I can freak out a little when something goes wrong, and he is steady. Something I think about a lot is how he didn't give up when it took me so long to warm up to him. And how it usually takes some time for me to warm up again when we go so long between visits.

But when we are together in the same room, or across the state, I'm finding he brings out the most loving version of myself that I had always wondered would be embraced if I shared it. And when I share it, it's appreciated.

He even called out, "You are so precise."

I'd heard this before and prepared for the rest of the thought, a put-down, that I should just speak in simpler terms... but then he said, "It's one of my favorite things about the way you talk," and I felt a weight lifted from my chest.

I can only hope that one day, when he's gone, because first loves don't last forever, that I love myself as much as he loves me right now.

2009, age 18, New Orleans

I fly out from SF and he from LA, and we meet at the airport. We roam around and the simplest things feel so much fun: walking down the streets lined with live jazz musicians playing and offering us lemonade in the street. Exploring where the levee broke. Having a Po' boy crocodile sandwich just to see what it's like. A swamp tour that was literally only fun because of his banter and jokes. Him posing with a little fake crocodile hand poking out of his sweatshirt. I could fall in love with him if he keeps doing things like that. Looking at me that way. Putting his hand on the small of my back the way he does. Seeing me so fully, and not looking away.

At one point, he decides to play. Seeing him play his sax in the French Quarter. I'd never considered the saxophone sexy until I heard him play it. I look at him and my eyes go soft and I just listen. Just feel. He brings out a simultaneous 'lost and found' in me. We even participate in Mardi Gras. Kind of. Me lifting my lips to reveal a full-toothed smile. I get a bunch of beads. So many that they actually feel heavy and you could barely see my neck anymore.

"You don't have to take your top off, all you have to do is smile!"

There ends up being only one bed in Louisiana when we visit his brother. But we mostly just cuddle. On our last night, something is different. He gets quiet, like he wants to say something.

"I. Love. You." Staccato in their spacing as though to emphasize their meaning.

A sigh of relief, combined with the swelling of bittersweet, overcomes me. I look vacantly into his brown eyes until all I can see is the pure black of his pupils; and I feel it. I feel that feeling. The one that can't tangibly be described unless through a metaphor or a simile.

It is an unanticipated gust of wind greeting your face, glistening from the sun's heat. It's like a shelter-providing cave that you don't mind being lost in. It's like writing an abstract, cheesy, lovey-dovey recount of something that *actually* happened to you, and now you can *actually* believe in it.

There's a nervous energy in the air and he takes a bit more space.

We are sitting on the deep chocolate brown couch, which is as stiff as a block of wood, hands clasped hopelessly in our laps. The sunlight has peered through the crevices of the poorly crafted curtains of only a slightly opaque sheet, red sweatshirt, and a handkerchief encrusted with musical notes. The light dances upon the white walls in a taunting manner, because all we really want is to be alone and lost for a few more moments in the dark of the night.

He tells me what he's going to say before he even says it. "When I first met you, I thought, 'I need to get to know this girl better,' followed by 'I think that you could be the one.'"

A light-hearted, heart-warming statement that puts "the one" and "me" in the same sentence? I silently ask myself in a state of dumbfoundedness and bittersweet bliss.

Then he nervously asks me, "Do you know what I'm going to say?"

I nod and wait. Tears swelling because I know within a few short hours he will be gone, but those words will stick with me.

Those last words are slightly quieter than the rest. As unexpected, yet fitting as any words could be in that moment with the moonlight peering in on a calm winter night. I feel in shock. And maybe like I do too? As in, love him, too? I only recently entertained the idea of falling in love with him. Isn't "I love you" beyond that? I can get there. I will, and with that split-second logic, too much time has already passed.

I say, "I love you too," and he holds me close and I feel a heaviness in my body. Did I lie if I know it's destined to be true? I've never been in love before. Is this what it feels like? This feeling like I'm going to throw up, and my knees get weak and I trust fall into him all of the time, sometimes for fun and other times because I can't help it. I just have to catch up.

He's always a couple of steps ahead of me. It's like he plans this and I don't have a plan. Should I have not said it? I can't take it back, and I don't want to. I don't know what he means by "the one." He wants to marry me? But what if I want to see what it's like to date more than one person? Is this puppy love? Is he just infatuated? Does he mean it? I have to let time tell.

"Actions speak louder than words," my mom says. And we embrace until we fall asleep.

2009, age 18, Novato, CA

I feel a ringing in my ears and my vision is blurred as a sharp pain runs from the base of my spine up through my skull. My twin brother Thomas walks by, and I know it was him, but how? He's a big guy, taller than Dad but lankier, with a wide grin. He used to get teased about his large ears by my dad. One time he got a piece of corn stuck up his nose when we were seven and had to go to the ER to have it removed since it was obstructing his ability to breathe.

A pair of scissors in his grasp and I still cannot speak.

Stunned. Sitting. Will I be okay?

I was just sitting down at the bench at the long knotted wooden dining room table, having dinner, when I asked my twin brother Thomas to move so that I could see the TV. I don't often watch it, so it seemed to be a small favor to ask. He ignored me and I repeated myself more loudly until he got up silently. He walked past me, and then the ringing.

After he walks past me with a red face and tight jaw, he's already in the other room and I feel the base of my back; no blood, only a sore patch of skin where the scissors were jabbed, right above my seat, right on my spine. We are adults now, although we still live at home. It's like my parents want or need us here, afraid of empty-nesting despite there being still quite a few kids to go through 'til that happens. My two sisters are fifteen and twelve, and my little brother is nine. Anyway, my twin brother and I, we are eighteen, technically adults, and we use our words now. Or should. I dizzily stand up from the chair and take my phone into my room. I'm not going to Mom and Dad as a grown ass woman.

With my heart racing, head throbbing, sore spine, I dial. 9-1-1. *What am I doing?* I think to myself. *Do you think they'll actually help you? Do you actually need help? You will get in trouble for this.* And then another side of me contemplates, *But this is wrong. He cannot just get away with stabbing you. You can walk, but what if something is wrong? You are scared and you have every right to be.*

The operator answers, "9-1-1, what's your emergency?" "My brother just attempted to stab me with scissors." "Where did he stab you?"

"The base of my spine."

"Are you safe now? Do you feel afraid?"

"I don't know. I don't know what it was all about. It was so unexpected and I don't know if he would do it again, or something worse."

"Has he been violent with you before?"

"When we were kids, sure, we both were. But now, he seemed so angry. The kind of angry that has been pent up for a long time. I don't feel safe."

"Okay, we can send someone over there to make sure it's safe."

"Okay," I breathe deeply, deciding to be curious about what happens next. I don't think I am overreacting. This is some Jerry Springer shit. I mean, come on. Who stabs their sibling with scissors as an adult? I thought it was over, this type of life.

When I hear the car pull up, and look out the window to see two uniformed officers walk to the door, it's the first time I've seen that exact scene but felt differently. I still feel anxious, and scared, but intermixed with a sense of ease now. I know that I am staying in this house when they leave.

When they come to the door, I hear my dad yell, "Shit, Stephanie. What the fuck did you do? He's going to the academy (police academy). He can't have this on his record. Selfish. You are going to pay for this if you fuck anything up for him, Stephanie. You've really done it this time. Fuck!"

I walk over to speak with them at the door.

My dad walks out and says, "Hey, I'm a retired police sergeant, I'd like to speak with you first and tell you what the situation is."

They look perplexed.

"I made the call, and I would like to request speaking with you first," I interject. One is speaking with me, and I try to concentrate on what happened, until my brother walks out.

With a pleasant demeanor and dopey smile, he waves like an elementary school teacher. "Hey, guys? Anything I can help with?" He starts talking with one of the officers.

I regain my focus.

"Will he do this again?" the officer asks me.

"I don't know. I wanted to call to ensure it wouldn't happen again. It's hard to know if something will become a pattern, and then when it does, how many times before it's finally not okay. These things can't always be chanced. We are all adults in this situation."

"That is enough," he says.

I feel a sinking feeling, like calling them is less about getting justice for myself, and more about creating more problems for me...then I hear my dad come out, and he pulls them each aside, walking farther down the hill for privacy.

I walk toward the front door and turn into the hallway, and press my head up against the screen door.

"She's crazy," I hear as he grows more animated. "She's not well. She has a history. I am sorry she got to the phone and bothered you. He didn't do anything wrong. He never touched her. She is delusional..."

And it's quiet. I assume they are nodding. I hear them go back to their car without another word, and drive away.

My dad walks in with a sigh, and I can hear him say, "Thomas, you did nothing wrong. She's just fucked in the head. You did nothing wrong. Good job."

I take a step out of my room as my brother leaves, and look at my dad with conviction and the calm and even tone I know he respects. "This isn't okay. None of this is okay. Nobody is allowed to hurt me. Nobody is allowed to hurt me now."

"Oh, shut up. I still have to figure out what to do with you. You can't pull shit like this." Dad shakes his head vehemently.

There's nothing left to say. I go back into my room.

— —

Benjamin's mom, Ann, has short salt-and-pepper hair and glasses, wears Clark's brand comfort sandals like me, and a corner office to the side of the kitchen with knick- knacks where she tracks estate sales and sells things on eBay for a profit. We don't talk much, but she invites me over for dinner sometimes and she's an amazing cook. Sometimes I'm not sure if I like it because it's different from what I grew up with, but I quickly decide this is how people eat who eat better than I have: steak is more medium instead of well- done, and baked russet potatoes are replaced with things like couscous or potatoes au gratin from scratch. She went to an Ivy League school where she met her now husband, who appears to be the yin to her yang. He is more upbeat and happy, almost a supporting character in the household if it were a play, while I can see a moody side of her, an intellectual feminist. I don't know her well yet I have a fondness for her, if only because she gave birth to my boyfriend. A gratitude that feels inherent for what I get to experience because she made the decision to have him. Now, in a way, I get to have him and he gets to have me.

2009, age 18, Novato, CA

"You'll always be pure," Benjamin says, holding my hands and gently locking eyes with mine as we sit on the sidewalk, with a softness and conviction that pierces through a primary parameter of my reality.

And I sit there, stunned. In plain awe of the truth of that statement.

Here I am, sitting on the sidewalk, embracing someone, another virgin, who is trying to tell me about how purity and sex can coexist. Purity of spirit? Seems too abstract to be valid. How can I still be pure after we do what we've been talking about doing? It seems to conflict with everything. If we have sex, I'd cross over into the gray area, excluded from the 'pure club' that was unarguably where I reside by this society's standards. If we have sex, I'm giving something up, my self-concept that I can control, what I do or what I don't... and should you only give in if you feel an uncontrollable need to, or simply because you want to? The latter seems like a waste, considering the amount of willpower I've honed.

2009, age 18, Woodside, CA

Benjamin's family friend, a couple we had dinner with, like a triple date with his parents, invite me and him to their ranch for a weekend over the summer. They are kind and I can tell that the wife is a little bit sassy like me and we see a bit of each other in one another.

Benjamin and I go on hikes, help out with yard work, and even find a private cove where we get to skinny dip, with the sun reflecting off of the water and our bodies. I don't think I've felt so free in a moment shared with someone else. I sort of think this would be the perfect place to do it.

We are having some arguments, they're not big, but just annoying, it's not seamless. He seems more irritated with me and me with him, but the love is there and maybe we are only now more comfortable with one another to share what could be better.

The first night I think he'll make a move to progress things, and he doesn't. The next night is our last night there and I'm giving all the signs and it's like he doesn't get it. I know that asking will kill the mood, but I bring it up anyway to confirm, and it does. I feel a sense of disbelief and anger. I know he's losing it too, and wants it to be special, and respects both of us wanting to wait, but seriously, it's been years. How much longer? What the fuck? I go to sleep and accept it. There are some things we just don't talk about, and this seems to be one of them.

2010, age 19, Novato, CA

He taught me to ride a bike with the patience and enthusiasm I didn't experience the first time my dad tried to teach me. I'd resigned myself to never learning years ago and, and it surprised me that when he asked if he could teach me, and I double checked that he actually wanted to, he said "Yes." After all, I kind of needed to know in order to go to college at UCSB, the biking capital of colleges.

"Hey, Stephanie, you've got this!" he'd call out with his arms outstretched and a wide grin.

I would bike toward him, and fall to be helped right back up. There was a supreme sweetness to this dynamic, bordering on saccharine. Why did he care if I knew how to ride a bike? Why was he being so nice to me? How could someone be this patient, really? He is something special.

— —

Ann stands in front of me, leaning forward, inches from my face. "I told him that someday some girl was going to love him, but that I was here first." Her fiery tone is muffled by an apparent desire to maintain composure.

We're in a meeting that I initiated, because I noticed that his mom doesn't say "hi" back when I say hi, or look me in the eye, and sometimes insists my boyfriend go outside by himself to do yard work when I arrive to spend time with him. We probably just need to clear the air. I look to him to stand up for me. He's silent.

I bite my tongue and let the thoughts that come to mind first pass, holding his hand tighter. "I don't think your son is replaceable."

A few moments too late, Benjamin reiterates, "I don't think she's replaceable, either."

"I'm just curious if there's anything I did, or any reason why there seems to be distance. I'd like to get along with you," I offer.

"I don't believe there's anything wrong and I'm sorry if you feel that way... I did hear about you going away to have a baby in high school, though. Not many mothers would want that for her son."

Feeling cut off from the emotion I could indulge in — this woman doesn't know me at all. And doesn't want to know me.

Believing gossip instead of the human in front of her. A deep sigh of disappointment contrasts her momentous tone. I hang in there, if only for a chance to preserve my relationship. I can feel the emotions later.

"Well, I went to boarding school... but that's impossible. There's no way I could have been pregnant at that time. Absolutely none," I state, hinting at my virginity.

"I guess it's none of my business, but how long were you gone for?"

"Nine months."

The room falls silent. So, she thinks I'm a slut. I know Benjamin believes me, and that's all that should matter. At this time, we've fooled around, but are still technically virgins. I'm not corrupting him; he's making advances toward me, but still, being this deeply misunderstood by someone who is so close to my lover, stings. It's like I'm looking at the thing that will break us, as he holds my hand lightly and does nothing.

— —

Tears streaming down my face in the bathtub. Blood tinting the water pink.

It hurts less than I thought it would. Resigned to what's happening.

So, although I know nobody would approve, I don't ask anyone's permission, or for anyone's opinion, and I do it myself.

Taking it slow until I jolt, not wanting to be present for this moment, resigned to a task I feel I must do, to be on the other side with pleasure, later.

I wanted it to be him, or somebody who loved me. More blood in the bathtub, pink streaked with red.

And a rawness I'm sure will heal by the time I see him again for his birthday. At least it's done so we can both enjoy it now. I'm ready to not tip toe around it or be in pain during it and he had his chance so many times and now it's like a flip has switched. I want it now. I wanted it months ago, but the timing didn't feel right to him? It's like my desire is a deterrent.

I have to please myself then.

Or at least get the displeasing part over with.

If he notices I don't bleed and thinks I cheated, I can honestly say I didn't, and feel at peace no matter what stories he makes up. But he knows me better than that, to think I'd be disloyal. Unless you count this as disloyal. This just isn't how I thought it was going to be. Bleeding alone in my bathtub.

There's no going back. It's done.

2009, age 19, San Francisco, CA

We stay in the city to celebrate his birthday and I feel like I kind of have the onset of a fever, but I wouldn't miss this. We finally do it. He's all smiles like he just won a prize. We watch TV like we usually do, and I feel cuddlier than ever. He, alternatively, makes little eye contact, and seems more interested in the TV than me. I feel my heart sink down into my stomach, into my legs, down into my feet, and slide right out of my body. I'm looking at him and he won't look at me. I don't feel like I can speak. I don't know what to say. I'm afraid. He doesn't see me. He's absent, and I feel like maybe the only way I can be safe is to be absent, too. The warmth, love, and caresses, they are absent at this moment, and I don't know if I've made a horrible mistake by going too far. There's no going back from going all the way. The next morning, he leaves as he always does, and I cry as I usually do, but this time with more riding on it than ever before. I feel like I have given something to him that he's pocketed, and that as my feelings strengthen, I can feel his waning. My enthusiasm toward him, ehem, towards "us," is becoming the thing that is resulting in me getting less and less of him. He told me I was "the one" several months ago and I was cynical, and now, as I'm starting to believe it, I can feel his apathy and distance.

His love certainly isn't deepening.

2009, age 19, Novato, CA

We've become a real couple now. We go out to dinners and have four to eight-hour video chats where we get into adult territory to hold us over until we can meet again in person.

Yet, when he's back this time, he's not the same. That spark, the eagerness to get to know me, and be close and explore has gone away. All he wants to do is sleep.

What happened to his energy?

— —

Then he signs us up for a salsa class in Hamilton. It's obviously usually for older couples working on reinvigorating the spark, but hey, if we fit that bill minus the age factor, so be it. He's very patient with me, and we begin to get the hang of it and have fun. I usually dress a bit corporate from my part-time admin role, but one night, I get creative.

I pack a red dress and stilettos in my bag, and arrive with my hair in a low bun and flats. I casually use the restroom after our dance class, and come out with my hair teased, red lipstick on, and a slinky red dress. I am READY for dinner. "Hi," I say casually, with a sultry smile.

"Hi," he says without emotion or expression, like he doesn't want to give me the satisfaction.

But I am his girlfriend — why wouldn't he celebrate how I look when I put in extra effort? I feel myself deflate, and feel like saving more of my creative ideas for another man someday.

2010, age 20, Novato, CA

Back in Northern California, in Marin, the weekend of my twentieth birthday arrives, and on a Saturday morning I walk my dog as usual. I notice a familiar car. I try to place where I've seen it before and realize it looks a lot like Benjamin's. Well, he's in LA, and I'm six hours away, so I'm probably just experiencing a Michelle Branch, "Everywhere to Me," moment. I carry on, and I can't get the thought out of my head. I don't memorize license plates, but damn, that empty car looks a lot like the car I'd spent so many rides in with his right hand on my left knee, and beyond.

I continue my walk down the private street, through the windy country roads, into the trail, and then back. The car is still there. And as I get closer, I see him. Benjamin pops out from behind the car and opens his arms to embrace me. I walk over and feel my heart flooded with light, and my knees start to soften as I allow myself to fall off balance a little and sink into him.

He walks over to his trunk and says, "I got this for you."

It's a princess cake, the kind I mentioned to him once, that I'd always wanted with pink almond frosting and a white cake and chantilly cream and raspberry jam filling, with a marzipan rose in the center and *Happy birthday Stephanie,* around it. He got it just for me. I don't know anybody who would do that for me, and I'm stunned, in silence. I want to cry tears of joy. Tears of confusion. Tears of gratitude. Tears of remorse.

"I didn't tell my mom I came... can I stay with you?"

I'm living at my parents' house after graduating college and Benjamin has been out of school for a year now. The whole 'get a job lined up right after college' didn't work out, despite my best efforts. It was either too early or too late. I took time off applying for jobs during finals, because wouldn't that defeat the purpose? And then even after getting an internship within a few months, it was in Marin, so it made no sense to move to the city yet, then the next job was actually in Marin too. I just couldn't justify leaving for a minimum wage internship in my parents' county, or a part- time job also in their county. But at least I get to save up. When I get a job in tech in San Francisco, that's when I'll leave here, finally.

My parents know we're broken up, so I say he has to stay on the couch now.

No need to involve them in the drama, but they can probably tell what's going on.

He goes to sleep on the couch and when my mom goes upstairs, he visits me. Although I know my mom wouldn't have cared if he just slept in my bed in the first place, I want to appear decent, like I have a good head on my shoulders and not get her involved. He holds me and there are no words, and we embrace in the special way we used to. We're less fumbly now and more fluid. I can now feel the love that had gone away, and my body is gold. We fall asleep embraced and I feel like in this moment, my heart is safe.

The next morning, in the moments before fully waking, I realize I haven't covered any blemishes, or put on lip gloss, but I feel a lightness from the inside. It doesn't matter. He's looking at me like I'm light and I feel like he opens that in me.

To confirm this sentiment, I ask, "Do you think I'm prettier with or without makeup?"

He's quiet. I am also quiet, since I want an answer.

"No comment," he says, and I realize that he may not be as elevated as I had thought. Or maybe he's just not wanting to lie. Even though I feel prettier with makeup on, it would have been romantic if he found only love where I believed faults to be.

I continue to speak, rambling to build myself up in a way that makes me feel more confident. "I know my body isn't perfect, but I work really hard so that it can do what it can do, like running, and I wouldn't change anything about its appearance."

"There's always room for improvement," he whispers.

I know this is an indication of his self-esteem and not mine, but I let him have it. Technically, yes, there is room. It doesn't mean he's not pleased with my body, because it's really in tip-top shape from training for a marathon and doing hundreds of sit-ups and squats every day... but there's something else here I don't care to dive into... I don't know why he felt the need to point out that it could be improved.

We spend the day in bed. I play music loudly for sound privacy. We dance along to the music and with each dramatic lip-synced phrase like, "We've only got 4 minutes to save the world," Madonna says, we laugh. He spends another night because it's only Saturday, and I don't explain Benjamin's whereabouts to my parents anymore. It's not their concern; I'm twenty now!

2010, age 20, Santa Barbara, CA

When I break up with him, not to be confused with the break we took late last year, I mean it. I am hysterical. I value him and our connection so much, but he's not present anymore. He's here but not, but mostly not even physically here. I can't put my life on pause like this anymore. For someone who wanted me so much then stopped caring but wanted to keep the label, the illusion. "I never thought I could actually have you," he said to me once, and it felt like a stalker-y thing to say. How long has he wanted me? At what point did he 'have me'? Does he mean sexually or as an official girlfriend? I don't ask these questions because they are too much.

But when I break up with him, it's in person and hard and I don't know if I'll ever find someone I love as much or who loves me as much, but it's a risk I'm willing to take. The next day, he's somehow in my room. He left blueberries, fresh roses, soy milk, and chocolate on my doorstep with a card the day before. And now he's in my room uninvited and it feels so intimate. How long has he been here? I ask him to leave and he wants to talk, but it's already been said. I love how he is trying now, but I can't break up with him every time he stops caring and get back together when he's desperate like this. It isn't sustainable. I ask him to leave, and not come over again unannounced, and he says, "Okay."

2011, age 20, Novato, CA

There's a sweetness to him still, Benjamin. He's eager to please my parents and even plays basketball with my little brother Tyler. *He's going to be a great dad one day*, I think to myself, watching his excitement at Tyler making it into the hoop. We also go on more and more runs together.

He's beginning to get pretty fit now, but still doesn't finish the food on his plate and often encourages me to eat what's left. I'm also usually a faster runner than him, which makes sense because I train so much, however, I'm starting to notice him jogging ahead and maintaining a faster pace.

One day I couldn't help it. "Benjamin, can you slow down?" I ask, out of breath.

"You want me to slow down?"

"Yeah, we can maintain the same pace, but honestly, I like it better when I'm in front. Benjamin, everybody likes you — your family, my family— just let me have this," I say without thinking.

Looking irritated, he agrees, and as I hear his breath and steps behind me on the narrow trail, I wonder if this is actually even helping.

2011, age 21, Santa Barbara, CA

"You're checked out most of the time, we talk about being together and when we are finally, you ignore me, and your family will not accept me. I wouldn't ask you to choose between them and me, you deserve to stay close with your family, so I won't be in this. I love you, but I deserve a better future than this." I sob uncontrollably as though a whole tiny town with miniature green plastic people has all gathered and is throwing daggers and pellets at my heart all at once from all directions.

It's the breakup I was afraid of before we even met that was dragged out longer than I anticipated.

I can hardly breathe. I had been trying to see if he could do it. After our meeting I initiated, him constantly asking his mom, "Do you like Stephanie?" then reporting back to me each time he asked, that "She said yes."

And me laughing annoyedly, "She's going to think I'm self-consciously asking you to ask her that. I'm more concerned with how we feel about one another. Can you stop asking her?" But he kept asking and kept receiving the same answer.

That's the difference. I am aware when I'm disliked and don't try to fight it unless we had a different beginning and it's something I'm processing. I may clear the air with a direct question, and suggest good will if it matters to me, but if their mind is made up, I redirect my focus. The only time this fucks me up is if someone I was close with flips a switch, but as far as I know, the woman never showed signs of taking well to me.

"Actions always speak louder than words," Mom said, and I stand by it.

I would never ask him to choose between us for a variety of reasons, and this is one of them. I am not one to fuck with or get in the middle of other people's family dynamics; everyone deserves close and loving relationships. I also want someone who will take a stand for me, a stand for us, if that's what it comes to, no matter the source of disapproval. This is the experience I need to make the hard decision, to choose a new path since I see this one's end so clearly.

Calling out a girl from school he knows... "I'm jealous of her," to see if he can tolerate an imperfection that I would not tolerate within myself, which is also untrue so that if it does change his heart, I know it's not real and I'm still lovable. I don't typically get jealous because I rationalize they deserve what they have, just like I deserve to have a version of it even if I don't yet, and me being mad they have it first doesn't make any sense. It's like I couldn't handle if he has a distaste for me and it being authentic. The pedestal has been a comfortable place to be, but I'm afraid I'm no longer there anymore, anyway. A contrast from before as I open myself up to normalcy.

He is committed to being a presence in my life, and apparently this is what life is like after the chase. I don't see it getting better. I want to date other men and know what that's like. And it feels a lot like settling, to consider staying in this. And when I say these words with such conviction and anguish, he springs into action.

It's like he wakes up. He gets flowers (he'd never gotten them for me while we were dating). He gets my favorite fruits and chocolates. He shows up unannounced. He's erratic. And it's too late. I've heard it before, but now I know from experience. This is a great love. And it's always going to be imperfect when melding two lives together. But I have to take a chance on myself, and imagine that a greater love is out there.

To be consistently loved by a man. To have his family embrace my presence. In order for that to be possible, this has to be over.

Leaving this love is the biggest risk in love I have ever taken, on the same level as entering it was, I guess, as a first love experience being what it is. And I'm taking it for a chance at something deeper, fuller. I feel like it exists, but I just don't have proof yet.

3. BOARDING SCHOOL

2005

"The one who's all alone, the one who people talk about but no one knows"

- "Villainize" by Stephanie Thoma

2005, age 14, Novato, CA

"We're sending you away," my mom says, with her hands to her face and tears streaming. Dad is in another room waiting for her when she's done with me.

They've threatened it for a while. The way she says it, I know it's not for a few days or weeks or a month like it usually is. I haven't even done anything wrong yet today for the entire day.

"When?" I ask.

"In two days," she confirms.

"Why are you doing this to me?" I try to stay calm, but I'm livid. I want the answers and know that if I let this anger bubble up and take over, I might not even last the next two days here. I try to keep this in mind and it's so hard.

She continues, "We didn't want them to come take you in the middle of the night. That's what they do to some kids. You might have nightmares. We wanted you to know. We did a lot of research. We just can't take care of you. We don't know how to parent you. You're too hard. You're too complicated for us."

I'm still mad, but my energy releases from my body as a deep sadness takes over. "Why not try harder? Why are you keeping the other kids but not me?"

"You're different, Stephanie. I have to try to save my marriage and I can't do that with you here. This isn't easy for me, but we have to do it for the other kids and for us, so you can get better."

"I just can't believe it. How long?"

"There's no end date. You're fourteen now, and it could be four years."

"You want me to be away... for years now?" and I feel myself choking on tears that are getting stuck in my throat as I try to breathe through it all so that I can get the information straight. The feeling of being unwanted weighs heavily in my throat as the words force themselves out. All I really want to do is cry, but I muster the will to speak.

She continues, "We love you and want you to get better. We will visit you."

"It doesn't feel like it. It never feels like it. And why don't you just speak for yourself and not Dad? Why am I the only one who has to change? And I don't know if I want you to visit me. You're just getting rid of me."

"I love you, Stephanie. The decision is made. Everything is booked. And I think you'll like it there. Maybe they'll understand you there. You just have to promise you won't run away. Otherwise, we have to get them to take you sooner."

"I promise." I turn away, limply walking down the steps into the room that won't be a place I can go to for much longer. I've never run away. All I want is to stay. I call Auntie Jewel. She always knows just what to say. She says that she knew about this and helped choose, which makes me feel betrayed. She says she'll call me, write to me, and visit. That I may actually find I like it (I doubt it). It will be different, but different isn't always bad. But all the new things I've experienced have been. I am not the problem. We both know this. They'll learn this once I'm gone.

— —

A large man and woman came to the house two nights later. I can see them in the kitchen area, talking in a hushed tone. They are talking with my mom and dad for a while as I wait in anticipation of venturing into the unknown. My legs tense, jaw clenched, I shake my body so that I can move my limbs when they call my name.

I didn't pack any belongings because my mom said the dress code is very conservative because there are Mormons everywhere and it'll be easier to just buy new clothes there with staff. The woman looks at me and says in an upbeat tone, "Are you ready?"

"Yes," I muster as tears instantaneously pour and I feel like I'm being walked off of a plank into a dark sea filled with monsters.

We are in front of the house and Mom begins to cry, but holds back and hugs me.

My dad walks up to me, looking uncomfortable but happy, and kisses me on the forehead with a "Bye, Steph."

I'm loaded into the strange car. And get on a plane for the very first time. This isn't the way my first plane ride was supposed to be.

2005, age 14, Provo, UT

When I arrive at the boarding school, I'm getting used to things pretty fast. People are saying I'm too quiet, which I hate. My first Saturday there I learn how to walk with a horse like people in shows do. I got a horse named Samson, and it begins well. Then he briefly steps on my foot. He does not hurt me, but hopefully on Thursday I can get a new horse that I get along with better.

I am required to go to the local Kohls to buy new conservative and winter-appropriate, as in snow, clothes. Nothing skin-tight, no spaghetti straps, and so on. I scoff, realizing my mom would love that this has turned into a shopping adventure. I try to have as much fun as I can being taken by the staff to get a winter coat, and even see if maybe I can grab some things that aren't on sale. When I return with over $200 worth of clothes, sweatpants, thick puffy winter coats, mittens... a whole new wardrobe, they take all of it to iron on a label with the 5-digit number I've been assigned. There's something unsettling about having your name and a number representing you etched into each article of clothing you now own, permanently pinching the fabric in weird places at the nape of your neck or lower back. But I guess this is what clarifies laundry and is simply how things are done.

I learned my goals are to not isolate myself, and to talk with staff about my feelings every day for the next month, which ends on May 11. I get my first letter from my friend Linda who has been present through it all, but she's still living in our hometown. She listens and when I ask her about her life, she gets quiet.

"It's not as bad as yours," and somehow that ends the conversation.

Maybe we do have seasons where we give or receive more and I'm in the season where even if I had more to give, it's not received, so my friends get to be there for me. Linda's letter is short, but she's sick, so I'm still grateful she took the time. I'm sooo bored.

Other highlights are that Maria tried to run away. She's really suicidal and has cut marks all over her. Now she has to be in the ISU for two weeks. Monica fell off a horse and was kicked, so she is in the hospital. Miley has been in the ISU for her behavior all week, and Faith has been in the ISU which is not a surprise at all.

The ISU is where you can be by yourself to not be a bad influence. Which is the opposite of where they would want me. They want me to talk to people.

— —

It's kind of sad that Jem ended up in the ISU and we can't play cards tonight like we usually do as roommates. Jem is a tall, medium-sized Indian girl, who's a year older, she's fifteen but developmentally a few years younger, with short hair kind of like a Raggedy Ann doll. She wears bell-bottom jeans and tshirts with glittery logos on them and doesn't talk a lot, but we have something in common: we are each in a place we don't want to be, and making the best of it, in one another's company at least. A lot of kids are having different experiences than me because many of them used to do drugs. I guess you could say I did too if you count all the pills my parents made me take for years, but here because they "don't have to deal with me," I get to be drug-free and take some pride in being among one of their easier clients.

Tell me the rules and if I can understand them, sure. Why not? The fight in me is gone, you could say, or maybe I'm just not repeating the same things and expecting another result. I am redefining what it means to "stay in it" for myself and am not sure how to describe it yet. I wouldn't do things like Jem did to get into the isolation unit (ISU) maybe when I was ten or eleven, but not anymore. I can think things through more now. What am I even fighting for? Like Aunt Jewel said, maybe this is in some ways better than home.

Speaking of which, I also had my first family meeting over the phone. At first I didn't talk because I couldn't stop crying. But then I managed to speak and the first thing I said was, "Have Amelia and Linda called?" I hope that made my mom realize how important my friends are. I don't say a lot, but when I do, it's about what matters.

I also discovered I have to wait two months until my mom can visit. Only 6 more weeks till June 5 (omg!!!)

I'm also finally a Level 2. I have not been assigned 3 months of taking chances every day, which ends July 21. I got bumped up to Level 1 and now can do my first extra activity, which is a movie at the library: Angels in the Outfield.

— —

I got my goals book and had a situation with Jem overreacting and lying about me. She said that I said something that I did not say that I don't even remember anymore, probably a misinterpretation and now she's offended and I'm in trouble. But at least I know what I said or did not say, and what I meant or did not mean. I understand myself and that counts for something. It sucked and now I feel uncomfortable in the same room as her.

I want to just go to my room but have to interact with peers and show leadership instead. We had a Friday slumber party, which was actually really boring. It ended at 2 in the morning so I only got 6 hours of sleep, which is unfair. They should have let us sleep in.

It's Saturday, my dad's birthday, so I called and left him a message "Hi Dad, it's Stephanie, Happy birthday." *click*

— —

"You're just a bit misunderstood, aren't ya?" Mel asks. She has tight blonde braids, drawn-on eyebrows, was once in the military, and it shows. She's strong, but rough around the edges. She's in her mid-twenties, and you can tell she gets a kick out of telling us what to do. She argues with some of the girls here, in an "I'm-your-big-sister-and-I'm-right-or-at- least-have-all-the-authority" sort of way.

When anyone asks to use the bathroom, she says that if you hold it long enough, your pee cycles back through your body. She had to learn that during her training. Even if you really have to go, you can hold it until you physically don't have to go anymore.

"Yes," I say in a whisper without making eye contact.

"Did you just get mixed up in the wrong stuff? You seem so... normal."

"The wrong family, we just don't get along and I don't bend over backwards to make it all okay," I correct softly, and know she shouldn't be talking to me like this but feel grateful she is. It's validating to be in a situation where you feel out-of-place and people don't think you belong either — something that can be agreed upon amid the madness of it all. But where do I fit? A fleeting thought without an answer.

Another time in the kitchen after we've made cookies, Mel pulls me aside, whispering after shifting her eyes back and forth as we sit behind the counter, everyone else in the common area. She seems genuinely concerned and excited, like an FBI agent who has cracked a code, but isn't sure I'll be able to implement it, and my interest is piqued.

"You just have to be smart. Don't give in if they taunt you. You're smart, you can think of it like that, outsmarting them." Mel says in another hushed tone that she shouldn't be saying, but I'm grateful she is.

"Easier said than done. When things happen, I feel like I can't stop. Can't stop the words I want to say from coming out. They just come out because I think I'd go crazy to keep them in, but they cause everyone to hate me. They would like me if I would just be quiet, but I can't. I don't want to when I have something to say at home, but at school, it feels so easy to go all day without saying anything."

— —

"You just put your hands around your neck so hard and forget everything," Stacey says.

All the kids have done it, and even still do it in their rooms. They cut off their air supply on purpose so they can pass out. People die from it, they say, but it's worth it because it feels so good. I mean, live and let live (or die, I suppose) but I'm not even curious about this. It's like sniffing glue or white out, or cutting their wrists, which are other things people here like to do, or at least do as an escape. I feel normal here, not to be confused with fitting in. It's more of a contrast. My quirks are less pronounced around all of these creative coping mechanisms other kids have adopted. While people are choking or cutting their bodies, sniffing things they shouldn't, I write. No judgment, it's just different.

I do make some friends, though. There's Miley, who's the same age as me, from LA, and talks about having been in a gang. She has already had sex and says her boyfriend has killed someone, and how she isn't allowed to wear her colors, but she still wears red handkerchiefs around her jean belt buckle the staff doesn't notice. She has stringy long brown hair, an olive complexion, and exclusively wears Abercrombie pants, is unfiltered, and says the funniest things.

She reminds me of the girls from juvenile hall, probably because of the way she wings her eyeliner and lines her lips in older photos of herself and she says she's been high. And there's the fact that she has also been there, in juvenile hall, and seems shocked that I have too, but respects it. She's in the bunk bed above mine. She will stay up all night laughing, then tell me why she's laughing and I'll laugh too. We tell one another secrets and I know she respects that I've also been in "the hall" but I don't elaborate on why. It somehow feels less badass and more... something else when your parents wanted you there.

We're the oldest girls in the "little girl" unit for eleven-to-fourteen-year-olds. My birthday is this year, August thirty-first, and I'll be fifteen. I wonder if they'll graduate me to another unit after I'm technically not among the youngest anymore. But something about it is soothing. I like being babied, and also feeling like the older sister while I am here. A role that's familiar, yet on pause, or nonexistent through all of these places I have been finding myself in over the years.

— —

Another friend who's like a little sister is Chantal. She has braces with rubber bands and an excessive amount of saliva that collects when she speaks. She is overridden with anxiety and often seen pensively smiling. I feel a sort of little sister quality within her and also a slight aversion to her learned helplessness and victim mentality, always being so hard on herself for the smallest issue. There's a comfort in being around somebody who cares so much what you think; I'm simply kind to her and aware of a sense of effort I never cared enough to hone myself, to please those around me. There's a sweetness that sometimes is saccharine.

Other than that, there are girls I'm friendly with, like Monica who's overweight and was on the diet meal plan and also has the same cussing, tight pants, winged eyeliner and dark lined lips thing going as Miley, but our talks never go very deep. But we walk around during breaks sometimes and just talk about current things, like school, what was for lunch or movie night.

Or Stacey, who reminds me of a friend I had when I was 7, and sometimes I listen to her talk about her relationship with her mom and although she never asks about me, I don't mind. It's nice to feel wanted as a sounding board. To get to be the person who listens to problems instead of the one who is the problem.

— —

I'm introduced to my therapist, Alanis. She is in her late twenties, has medium-short dark blonde hair in a deep side part, with pearl earrings and a pearl necklace to match. She has bigger lips and a bigger nose than I would initially expect to see on her pale, partially freckled face. She has a large gap between her eyebrows and wears boat neck blouses and pencil skirts and looks professional. She tells me about how she used to pick her nose when she was my age and asks what habits I have that I could be embarrassed about. Like this will make her relatable and make me want to open up to her. However, I'm too busy thinking about a grown ass fifteen-year-old picking their nose, with a sense of curiosity and repulsion, to get too deep into my own quirks.

She has me take an assessment consisting of questions that reflect my inner state and how understood I feel or not. When the results come back, she shares that I'm "definitely disturbed," and says that I shouldn't worry though, because my score can change and they'll retest me often. She shares she has a special knack for "helping kids get back on track to revere the people who brought them into this world." She can tell I don't respect my parents, and shares that she too had less respect for her parents when she was my age than she does today, but now that she is a parent, and an adult like they are, she loves them more than ever. She was wrong, and they were right. And I am so lucky to be here because I won't have to wait so long to realize this like she did.

I realize how this is going to go. There's only one way out of here, if at all, before I turn eighteen. Good behavior. And I know it'll be easy to keep my cool. I feel like I can control my emotions a lot better than I used to. Ever since getting to Utah I cry sometimes but am otherwise pretty numb, but in a happier kind of way. My period stops the whole time I'm here, maybe it's because of stress my mind can't process. Some kids get in trouble for complaining about this place over the phone or in letters. I know I'm always being watched — every spoken and written word — and don't see the use in complaining, anyway. There are some ways in which this place is better than home, I rationalize. My parents agreed not to have medication forced on me anymore, after I had pleaded for years. They say now that I'll be in expert care, my mood swings should be monitored and not get to the caliber of when I'm at home. The thing is, I don't have mood swings here. I don't know how to get angry anymore, really. If someone says something I don't like, it rolls right off. I was sent here for anger, and since they are not seeing any signs of uncontrolled anger (without the catalyst) they focus on my social skills instead. I need to talk to people more, apparently.

I never had issues at school, but now they are saying I actually did, by not talking enough.

They may think I'm faking this calmness, but the catalyst of my anger isn't here. I'm realizing it's not the city, or the house, or the place. It's the people. The people who I feel most misunderstood by aren't here, and I don't expect people other than my parents to understand me well, so if they do it's just a nice surprise and if they don't, I'm not angry with them over it. In some ways I can relax while I'm here, and in others I have new stressors — the opportunity to have my behavior not just "good" or "bad," but quantified. In a new system with enough structure to resemble an elaborate jungle gym, domesticating the wild teenagers by taking them out of their natural habitats, and into cohabitation with one another, with the sole intent of reforming them and their natural tendencies. I am an observer in my own life; taking notes, noticing details in the way those around me dress and present themselves to the outside world. Their facial expressions and how they feel. Sure, some things annoy me at times, but instead of that fire that would boil up at home, it's more of a flicker that quickly dies out, as something like a cool breeze blows it out like it was never even there.

While meeting with Alanis more and more, she sometimes asks me point-blank if I agree with her. She's pretty transparent that she is in regular contact with my parents, and how they enjoy my phone calls each week, as I suspected. I wonder what else they say or ask. I know whatever I say is being relayed to them, there is no protection, certainly not here with this woman whose life mission is to "set kids like me straight."

I take the test again after a quarter, or three months, and I'm "better." Still "signs of delusion," but "better."

"Do you think I'll get to a place where I'm no longer delusional?" I ask, with an internalized smirk. I wonder who these people are who decide the testing for who's crazy and who's sane. I'd like to meet them and see how sane *they* actually are.

"It's so deeply rooted, it's unlikely, but I do think one day you can be a functional member of society."

She's always asking me if I can see my parents' perspective, but not if they can understand mine, which is code for, "Do you agree with them? Have you realized yet that they are always right and you're always wrong?"

At first I am my usual defiant self and refuse to see their side, trying to be understood instead, but then I realize they may never have compassion for me, but I can cultivate compassion for them. So, in my own mind, I decide that my viewpoint is still valid, but no longer speak about how valid it is with her. Instead, I give a voice to my parents' perspective that I can understand better than I could when I was younger. How good their intentions were, and how I could have done things differently at home, been less reactive regardless of the catalyst, while holding my full reality deep inside.

— —

I went on a hike to the "Y" at Brigham Young University where all the Mormons go to school. It took about one hour and ten minutes. I asked my mom what I got on my Meyer's test; I'd like to know how my personality is doing. I went to the bean museum and saw dead stuffed animals and felt a live tortoise and boa constrictor. It wasn't that much fun.

I spoke with Dad briefly and I wonder if he's happy I'm gone. The call with my mom was awkward since she said "I love you" and I was silent, then we hung up.

The family therapy meeting over the phone left me feeling misunderstood by my mom and like I need to improve my communication skills PRONTO!

I'm feeling like the new girl Kathleen is fitting in better than me and people like her more. She is from the South with a short blonde bob, some teenage acne, and a drawl that matches the drawn-out intensity of her big blue eyes. You can tell she is intent on making a keen impression, and she does. I want to get to know people in my unit better and it's cool she can do that and make it look easy. Am I actually capable of that, though? I'm not sure I can or want to be that attuned to everyone else before I say a single word.

Monica is a rotund girl a year younger than me, with slicked back hair in a ponytail and lined lips and a cat eye. She's also in my unit, and is always asking questions, but not in a way that shows she cares, rather in a way that suggests she wants information to then share with others, who I also don't trust. She's been super nosey, so I plan to confront her appropriately, of course, when she says something like that again, asks about personal things like family drama or my sex life (that doesn't exist) which will probably be tomorrow.

— —

It's Mother's Day, so I called my mom but still couldn't say I love you, maybe on her visit it will feel normal. I have dark under eye circles, so I have been prescribed Hylexin to fix it. I had a dream that Mom and Dad died and woke up at 4am crying and it sucked. I also need to get my math grade way up, I feel overwhelmed. I wanted to stop taking all the pills but now could use some Zoloft. I moved rooms and Candi made a comment about her being on a low-fat meal plan and if I notice, like she wants me to assure her that she is not fat, although we are all getting plumper by the day here with what they feed us, and it's just uncomfortable.

NOT THAT SWEET

— —

My goal is to have a conversation for fifteen minutes each week with someone I don't know. I got bumped back to a Level 2, this happens all the time, and it sucks. We are rated 2x per week and it always changes if I am not perfect. I wonder if I can express emotion and have such honesty be celebrated. Sometimes I say it in a way they do not like. The family meeting went BAD, and it's clear I just need to listen to my family and my therapist Alanis 100% of the time. I won't go into details because I just want to forget about it. If I want this to work, I both need to socialize more but then also not talk in certain situations. We had a prom, and it was fun to dress up, but I didn't talk to any boys. It makes me think of the boy that used to talk to me in choir class. The last time I saw him he looked me up and down with his eyes and licked his lips, and thought to myself, *"he probably wants one thing."* He probably has a girlfriend by now, since it's been over a month. He probably wasn't good for me anyway, so I'm not missing out. We played the video game Disney Scene It, where you guess which movie scene the video clip is from and watched a half-hour of Finding Nemo.

— —

I got put on talking logs to ensure I am talking enough. I feel lonely and uncared for — it's not clear when it's okay to just be by myself and have that be healthy. I saw a play called Holes at BYU and had an enlightening talk with Jem about family curses and themes that follow families and good versus evil, and if that's even really real. Tani went to the ISU and is in isolation for now, so the room is being rearranged.

I cried about 4 times today, and my family call wasn't good or bad, which feels like progress.

"I will always love each and every one of you," Joanne says after reading another chapter of The Velveteen Rabbit Principles. Joanne is the leader of our unit and you can tell she takes a lot of pride as a role model. She tries to have 1:1 time with everyone and looks us in the eye — careful not to pick favorites. Joanne is in her late thirties or early forties, moderately fit with muscular calves that protrude out from her quarter-length pants. She has a perpetual rusted wine-rose lipstick-lined smile with a slight gap between her two prominent teeth I can't tell is genuine or etched onto her face despite pain. She and I both choose to believe it's real. She's openly single and encourages us to eat to our heart's content when cinnamon rolls are served. Seconds, even.

I saw Star Wars Episode 3 in a crappy movie theater, and was bitten by a horse named Simba, but it wasn't that bad. I went on the "zipper" ride at a carnival with Maria and had fun. They have this event called interfaith, and it's often pretty boring. I also went off campus to Hogi Yogi to get fro-yo and it was sooo good! I'm being told I don't always participate enough and need to get out there more and actively ask people to be my partner in games and more. The simple pleasures these days are off-campus trips to ColdStone.

Kathleen and Chantal are my favorite friends right now. I have calls with Mom each week and got feedback that I talk about going home too much. It's just always on my mind and I don't want anyone to forget that I want to go back and this place is not my first choice, but I'm making the best of it. It's not allowed. I understand, if I talk about it, then it gets other kids upset, or my parents get upset and it's not okay to say if I don't like it here or want to leave. I get it, but I still feel the way I feel. I'm feeling more depressed about being here for an undetermined amount of time, and how I keep trying to get to Level 4 for good behavior, and then it's a surprise when I get feedback that I'm not there yet — I wish they could tell me sooner so I could improve before there's a new thing to work on. It's really my purpose in life these days, the levels. Alanis said I should get a visit every six weeks since I asked about the maximum and that feels like a long time, but it goes by fast. We go off campus to play games and get snow cones and to celebrate birthdays. I went with Monica, Chantal, and Tani.

I ran six miles one day during free time, I counted all the laps. That is a record so far, and I think I want to do it again. I'm glad that I am also now saying "no" when offered things like s'mores as a casual snack. I don't even like s'mores if I'm being honest, but they can make you feel like things are more okay than being in silence and nothingness. Even so, I say "no."

— —

I start to count calories and notice a grandma's brand cookie is 200 calories each, even more if you eat the whole package. Candi leaves and everybody cries and I don't and I can see it bothers her, but it's just not my reaction.

Joanne asks me to help out and ask people to help me out whenever I feel like it. I'm not always sure when it's okay to ask or offer my help, when it's intrusive or welcomed. Here goes nothing!

I noticed I gained a pound since I started tracking my weight, something I am now more aware of.

I saw the movie Red Eye off campus and it was really good. I was in a horse show and tied for last place because they probably wanted everyone to feel like they won. I think the judge was unfair, but whatever this is not a big part of my life. I celebrated my birthday and my friend Nahmi said I have three to four gray hairs; I have earned them by age fifteen.

2005, age 15, Novato, CA

I get to go home for my fifteenth birthday. On a plane for the second time, Utah to California. I've only been here for four months, but apparently my parents miss me. We have a weekly phone call and there's a softness I can feel, like maybe we all look forward to it. And when I cry of loneliness and missing them and tell them that, maybe with my mom, she gets it. I don't talk like that with my dad because he won't care how I feel. I get letters every week from my two best friends, twins Amelia and Linda, that are opened before I read them, they are monitored and probably recorded or relayed to my parents, but uplifting nonetheless. My friends tell me to stay strong, that it's horrible I'm gone, but I'm strong and will get through this.

For the first time I can remember, my parents get me my own birthday cake. Usually it's half a cake, half for me, half for my brother Thomas. I experiment with putting self-tanner on while I am home, and streaking sun-in through my hair, to lighten it, and I look like an orange Oompa Loompa mess. I am beginning to get more of a figure with hips and boobs that are still small, but a little bigger (Mom always said I would be a C cup by the time I was fifteen, and nope, that's not where we're at but we're going in that direction). I wear a tight tie dye quarter-length sleeve top my mom got me for my birthday and my midriff shows a little when I wear it, and although part of me wants to pull it far, far down, another part lets the bit of skin show, knowing it will be an impossible sin once I return to Utah. The weekend is amazing. I am celebrated by my friends and parents, and everybody missed me and celebrates me. Maybe this is what it will be like when I'm an adult and only go home for a weekend every once in a while. My parents always insist I spend my birthday with them, and ya know, this one hasn't been bad. I liked it, enjoyed it, appreciated it- swimming at the pool in a bikini instead of the tankini I have to wear at boarding school, and spending time with friends who aren't also labeled crazy by society. It's something I could get used to, but I don't, because it's only for a weekend.

2005, age 15, Provo, UT

I have an empty feeling coming back to Utah after a trip back to California for my birthday. I got cake and to see my real friends that are not just made of convenience, and now I'm back, and I have no choice. I am doing my healthy eating more and more except for the night of Miley's fifteenth birthday. She is only one week younger than me.

All my goals for this month are:
- Take bigger risks

- Participate more in rec therapy
- Participate more in group therapy
- Show leadership by helping others, sharing ideas, and setting a great example

I'm "on A.p." which means I am under review for a level shift... with my visit in jeopardy, I'll do my best to maintain my visit, with God to help me. Are you there God? Help me out, please. It's about time. My parents don't believe in God, but I'm trying it out to see how I like it. I went to the Utah State Fair and ate Dominos. Went to Chilis another night. It seems like eating ice cream and movies are all there is to do around here aside from these activities. And knitting blankets while watching those movies. I made one with a soft blue, brick red and white yarn that's so big it will cover my parents entire king bed. And another one for my grandma that's smaller and her favorite colors of light pink, rose and white. We also go to Dairy Queen. The album that has the District Sleeps Alone Tonight on it by the Postal Service is on repeat in art class, and the vibe pretty much captures our time here. It's a year old but listening to it so many times in a row I have a newfound appreciation of it, from like to love, and my realism art looks a lot better than I thought it could.

I have a visit coming up and it's only 1 hour and 35 minutes away. Now at least I know my discharge date is moved to February, so that would give me 6 more months. In therapy with my dad, he points out negatives and says I don't accept feedback, as usual.

I am feeling dysthymic. Apparently I don't have depression, but a milder form of it, so I use this word now to describe it. My dad visits but it's delayed, so I continue life here wishing he was here sooner. My parents visit me separately for some reason they decided on without mentioning to me. Quality time maybe, where it's less like both of them ganging up on me. Dad and I end up going for ice cream and go on a hike of the Y, which is the Mormon college symbol. He's wearing a flannel jacket like he always does, but I'm not sure he was prepared for the snowfall. He seems to be happy exploring a new place. And there are moments when it seems we both are happy with one another. When I get back from my visit, I feel emotional and am amazed I'm still a Level 3 when I have been doing all they ask of me.

— —

Getting a donut at Glazies is the highlight. It's pretty much all except for being upgraded to a Level 4, finally! Ellen initiated a fight with me, then emotionally apologized, but I guess it's all ok because I was never caring much about the whole thing. I have my visit with Auntie Jewel and we overeat, and I decide I'll do my best to cut carbs when I come back. Halloween was a total pig out day. It's the only thing I can control, sometimes, what I eat, and I'm not doing a great job, to be honest. I can workout at least and keep running. I am having slices of bread and cinnamon rolls. I binged when they took us to all you can eat Dominoes, which I should have known better than to do. Fourteen slices of pizza.

— —

This place really encourages you to eat. Everybody looks overweight. They tell me to finish my plate, and what they feed me is good, but there's just a lot of it. After a few months, I start to get chubby too. I ask to be put on weight loss meals, since they are balanced and have more fruit and protein, but they say I am not eligible and that I am perfectly fine and healthy. I'm a 'growing girl.' As if sugar and fat were going to fix us rather than contribute to our diminishing mental wellbeing.

— —

We have one hour of free time, and one day, it's snowing and we're inside the gymnasium. I look over and see a couple of people walking around in slow steady circles, but most of all, people are sitting down talking. I feel the urge to move, fast. I run around once, then again, and I don't stop. I am huffing and puffing, and sweaty and when the hour is over, I go over to the water fountain gulping down replenishment and vow to do this again. Every day, we have free time in the gym. For the next five months, I run for around five hours per week, and can feel myself getting stronger and healthier.

2005, age 15, Salt Lake City, UT

We got to go to a demolition derby in Salt Lake City where drunk ladies screamed things like "Move your ass!" and "I'll show you my left one!" We get ot go on a field trip for Levels 4 and 5, those who are good or perfect in other words. I'm usually a 4 on an average day which means I am great, just not impeccable, and a 3 on a bad day which is horrendously average, if I speak up about something I don't like, for example, or become irritated about something and express it. Being a 1 or 2 simply isn't possible for me, as they are the bottom of the barrel, for people who aren't entertaining the rules clearly laid out. Basically, be quiet about the things you don't like — even if you say something in a respectful way, if it isn't value-aligned with what the person in charge believes, they'll thank you for your honesty and swiftly dock you. Sometimes my honesty is more important so I risk it, and can see it coming when I do, but not to the extent of a Level 1 or 2. It's for those who are less in control of themselves. You begin at a Level 3, like a neutral slate that isn't particularly good or bad, which can feel like a clean slate if you're used to being judged a certain way, and can go up or down from there, and I decide it's all up from here. So, we are in Salt Lake City at a monster truck show, and it's becoming more and more clear that Salt Lake City is NOT Mormon-ville.

People are drunk spilling their beers on us in the bleachers, wearing biker gear with tattoos, and some women are even flashing their bare chests, screaming "wooooo!" as oversized cars smash into, and eventually pummel over and flatten out, one another. You can hear the crunch, screeching of metal, and the energy of the crowd, and while I'm excited to be out, and experiencing a new city, I quickly determine this isn't my scene and I will not elect to go to one of these shows again. If anything, I spend more time watching the people in the stands, the people who like this. It's more interesting than the cars, more dynamic.

2005, age 15, Provo, UT

"You're not going to care about this once you get home. I know I shouldn't be saying this, but you really will not care at all and you will have moved on to other things," Brad, one of the new staff members says as I'm crying because I was demoted from a Level 5 to a Level 4 during my last week.

There would be no way to regain my status before leaving, since we're assigned levels weekly.

"That makes sense, but now it's all that matters. I worked so hard and didn't think I deserved it and now it's proven true," I say.

I think about the times when I convinced myself I didn't care what anybody thought. My parents. My siblings. People at school. How did I get here? To a place where what other people think matters so much more, and can build me up or otherwise? Or did I always care and now there's finally enough space to understand and express it?

— —

There was a dance, and I actually danced with a bunch of guys and 'let go,' and this shorter guy Dominick kept asking me to dance. Attended the Silent Nutcracker, and it was okay.

— —

Getting free… It's been almost nine months, early April to late December, and to my surprise, my therapist says with a smile, "Stephanie, you still have a lot of work to do, but after your third assessment, you are significantly more mentally healthy and less delusional than you were when you first got here. I mean, you still have a lot of work to do, but how do you feel about your progress?"

"It feels good to have progress," I share.

"Well, we could do more work together, but I'm excited to announce that your parents have said they are as impressed with your progress as we are, and they would love to have you home for the holidays."

"Oh, so for a week or two? Do you mean Christmas and New Years? Or only one?"

"Sounds like your obsessive thoughts are back, calm down... they want you to come home. You are discharged in one week."

When she says the words, I feel more calm than excited. I had mourned the possibility of a 'regular' high school experience, and was planning to make the best of the next three and a half years here until I became a legal adult, but another part of me knows that to really grow and feel normal, I need to go. They "want" me to come home. Just, wow. It's like a dream and I feel nervous and excited, and like I could cry. My parents want me home. I am wanted.

"I will gladly accept that offer." I smile, and I feel like I got a second chance at life.

4. YOUTH SHELTER

2005

"Those labels were never hers."

-"Villainize" by Stephanie Thoma

2005, age 14, San Anselmo, CA

"It sounds like people haven't been listening to you, and I'm so glad you shared your story with us," Janine says. She's a twenty-something year old woman who works at the youth shelter, asks why I am there, and I tell her. Everything.

"I am trying to just be myself and when I am my dad gets mad, and then they do things that push my buttons. They pin my siblings against me and call the police because they say I'm out of control when I'm only really out of their control..." I share, exasperated and afraid of the pending judgment that doesn't happen.

She maintains eye contact with me and even holds my hand. She listens. I feel a mixed sense of validation of my own sanity, but also wonder if we're both crazy. How can she understand that my parents, the hospitals, the police, are all wrong about me? That statement is bold. She hugs me and I retreat into the sensation of understanding, of being understood. She tells me about her issues with dating and her weight, and I listen and assure her she isn't fat. Even adults have insecurities like these. I've never really given much thought to my body- it's just there. Sometimes I feel like I'm not in it.

The place feels like a home. There are no bunk beds, only wooden frames and what look to be full-sized mattresses. Real beds. Windows that have trees outside of them. We wear our own clothes. Have outings like going grocery shopping where I get to help pick out ingredients for dinner and put them in the cart like I used to do with Dad. We also spend time cooking together and watching movies on the couch. I didn't really like "My Big Fat Greek Wedding" but I watched it twice just so I could sit next to the ladies who work here.

"Can I stay?" I remember asking Janine, full well knowing the answer. I'd been there for about a week, and it was so much nicer than the other places I've been. How it looked and felt. I was trusted and liked and heard. Although I didn't always like the food, or get to know my roommates well, it felt like a safe place to land. Perhaps what a group home would have been like... could have been like.

But this is a place for kids in crisis, and you can only be in crisis for so long, until you get into a rhythm of movie watching and grocery shopping, and it's time to go back. The soft place to land during a crisis situation did its job.

It's people like Janine, and Jewel that keep me going, letting me know that one day I could surround myself with people who, too, understand.

I am invited here only a couple of times, and I wish it was longer, so just savor the times I get to come.

5. JUVENILE HALL

2003 - 2004

"It's easy to 'villainize' a victim, who won't back down."

- "Villainize" by Stephanie Thoma

2003, age 13, San Rafael, CA

Into the handcuffs, into the cop car, duck down into the seat so nobody you know sees, stay quiet as the cops talk in code in the front seat, exit the car into the intake room, overhear the cops talking about how you're trouble, disrobe and take off all jewelry and shoes, put on what they give you, go into your cell room and wait.

Then it's time to visit the doctor here, in juvenile hall. A nice stout Hispanic man situated in a small sterile room with white walls and a chair like I'm at the dentist. He's giving me a TB test, which is mandatory here. The kind where a bubble forms under the skin of your forearm and if you don't have it, it goes back down, but if you do, it gets more inflamed and all kinds of nasty. If you don't use used needles, then you should be fine, they say. Considering I don't use any kind of needles, I imagine that I'm extra okay on this one, but he never asked me about drug use.

Then he asks about the last time I had sex. "I've never had sex."

"Even oral sex counts. Or anal." He looks at me with his chin downturned as though now my answer will necessarily change.

"I haven't had any type of sex before," I clarify, blushing and slowing my breathing so my face will feel less warm, while maintaining eye contact in a matter-of-fact tone. I recently turned thirteen. Who has time for that? It seems super contrived versus "natural" like people say it is. I cannot imagine letting someone mount me and finding that fun. But when you really like or love someone, you want them that close? I'll cross that bridge when I come to it.

"You know what... I believe you," he says, pointing his finger toward my face before he continues, "Wow... I mean wow!" he exclaims loudly, looking over at his colleague... "Hey buddy, she hasn't had sex before!"

"Really?" his colleague asks with wide eyes.

I sit silently. The doctor puts his hand up, elated, "Hey give me a high five! Don't start having sex. You are doing so well. You're ahead of the game on this one. I mean, wow... another high five!"

After I give him those two high-fives, not feeling the same level of excitement, my eyes glazing over at this false accolade of something I have not yet done, I'm informed that 'I made his job easier,' and can leave now. I'm done with tests. A fleeting thought... why do people care whether a penis has entered my body or not? Why is it 'good' that one hasn't? If people think that the 'bad kids' here have necessarily done it, but I haven't, this is a way to be 'good.' Sounds simple enough. I make a mental note.

— —

I observe a lot while I'm here. I don't feel scared, or maybe I just cut it off because I'm overwhelmed. Instead, I decide it can be like I'm a researcher in a place that isn't meant for me to acclimate to, but rather, get curious about. I met a guy named Jerome with tight ringlets and a full smile, but empty eyes in the common area during social hour in the room with pay phones, places for family visits, a tv for movie nights. Today is his last full day before he's discharged- not because of good behavior, or a maximum amount of time, but he's aged out of the system. He's here because he's stolen cars for a living, and sold them. He is turning eighteen tomorrow, and everyone, mainly male staff who've come to know him over the years and other delinquents, gathered around.

"I'll miss you, but I hope I never see you again," this one staff member said with a pat on the shoulder, then a tight one-armed hug.

"I'm just scared, man. I mean, I feel taken care of here. I get food. A roof over my head. A bed. But we're goin' into the big time now."

"Yeah man, if you fuck up, it's not gonna be like this, so nice."

"All I know how to do is fuck up," he says, on the verge of tears.

It's as though he wants to be hopeful, but he knows he'll only transition to the next level. The system is rigged like that, you know? You don't? Let me show you.

2004, age 13, Novato, CA

"Who Am I?" the worksheet reads. I'm in my 8th grade classroom. Homeroom. Fluorescent lights, multi-colored construction paper art on the walls, seated in a cold laminate desk with the standard wrap-around, faux-wood hutch holding the worksheet in plain view. The clock is ticking to my right, as each student filling those seats silently writes. I am in 8th grade English class with the kind of teacher that plays golf with some of his students on weekends, watches The Real World Miami, and is considered "cool." I stare blankly at the page, knowing I am expected to write a creative poem, limply holding my pen, feeling the weight of the question and all that I can say. Just as quickly as I envision that possibility, my mind is as blank as the page before me and I can't think of anything at all.

I end up sticking with the facts:

I am a daughter, a sister, a friend, a niece, a cousin, a student, a classmate.

That's who I am.

Relationships are a mirror for me, allowing for various forms of reflection. People on the other end of those titles, mom, dad, sisters, brothers, aunties, uncles, cousins, teachers, and classmates... their words, or what I imagine them to be, are what I am, by association at least. Sticking with these titles has a way of giving me context in the world and a sense of normalcy. Everyone can relate, even if it's only on the surface. It's safer there, anyway. And if the alternative is being crazy, evil, out-of-control, self-centered, manipulative, mean, the problem, a bad seed... wouldn't you prefer that former list too?

The teacher has us go around and predict what our fellow students will do for a living when we grow up. When it comes time, the guy who sits one seat ahead of me, Alex, proclaims, "Stephanie will be a playwright." And I wonder where he got that random idea, but I kind of like it. Maybe it's not all about who I've been, but who I can become.

2004, age 14, San Rafael, CA

I'm glad it's after dinner time so I can go to sleep. I eat white bread and butter at dinner, so it's not much to look forward to. For every meal. Everything else is disgusting. People have found bugs in their food, and I don't care to take my chances. One of the girls taught me this- the one that has thin winged out black eyeliner and tattoos, but when her makeup is off, she looks a little like me. The trick is to layer butter between the bread slices, and remove the crusts, then smash it into a ball and eat it from the middle. During the optional social hour, I go back to my room. Why would I go out and be social when I can just have some peace? "Soldier" by Destiny's Child blasts, and other rap songs will play until quiet hours begin at nine. Sometimes I wish I had a pen so I could write poetry, thoughts, or a story. But then I think it's better to forget, and if I had it written down, it would all seem too real.

"You just want everyone to feel sorry for you," my dad always says.

But that isn't even true. I'd rather just disappear and have nobody notice I'm here.

When I close my eyes, I could be anywhere. Not on this

concrete slab. Not in these strange clothes we wear 24/7. Not locked in a room. Not in my body. And I dream.

— —

I'm not sure how many times I walked along that track, or wrote with those small severely chewed-upon pens in the combined classes of all grade levels where I got a "B" no matter how much effort I put into a project, no matter the subject either which worked out for math... or how many painted white bricks I counted once they locked my door. Whenever I'm here, time stands still. I feel peaceful only because I'm not fighting to stay, or fighting to leave. I leave that to the others here, mostly boys.

There are usually twenty boys and maybe a few girls. Because of this ratio, all activities are mixed. When we have movie nights, they have rows of thick plastic chairs on one side of the room for boys and a small sliver of a row for the girls. Maybe it's 90-95% guys. At most there were seven girls at a time, but I have been the only one before. It's not like the girls here aren't tough, though. You can take a look at some of them and guess what they've done.

I can't walk around the track without a wolf whistle, claps, "That ass, though!" or an extended, "daymnnnnn!" from the older boys. Us in our orange sweatpants and sweatshirts. Fewer of us in worn Hanes bras and oversized crepe-like off white granny-panties. I have never feared they would do anything. I'm pretty sure I have a cool "don't fuck with me" face, even though I'm objectively pretty small. Not short, just slender. I feel oddly protected in a way, not by the guards, but something we can't see. I get to be good here, so I ease into it, relaxing into the feeling of what I always wanted to be.

NOT THAT SWEET

— —

One of the times I am checked in, after I replace my clothes with that orange Hanes uniform, I sit with another regular. She's an Asian girl named Lisa with bleach blonde hair and large, black-lined eyes. I once walked by as she was getting a pat down and saw her completely naked and noticed her boobs were way bigger than mine.

"Can you tell?" she whispers, looking at me holding back giggles.

"Tell what?" I whisper back.

"That I'm high as fuck!" She covers her mouth and muffles the next words, "They probably don't suspect it since it's during the day. Damn, they really don't know."

I've never been high before, so I don't really know either, but I congratulate her. "Yeah, I had no idea, just whisper more quietly, you're louder than you think." I caution. "You're good, though. Solid."

— —

When we go to school at the juvenile hall, no matter what age, fourteen through eighteen, we're all put in the same room. We get little pens with rubber tips that are so small they feel like Q-tips. Is this so they can't be used as weapons? Nobody is paying attention, and I'm trying to, but it's confusing to be learning one thing in school at home, then here they try to teach you something random. I'm usually here for one week or maybe up to a month. I think one time it was more than a month, usually when you have to wait for court.

Writing though. I love it. I do my best, and they give me a B on one of my papers. I try harder the next time, another B. I don't try at all the third time, and still, a B. They're not even reading it, I realize, and I also come to terms with the fact that being here is fucking with my GPA. I still write for 'fun' with a tiny pen on tiny pieces of paper, but rip it up once I'm done since I know they read everything here. I don't need my journal entries to become public knowledge, so I write, then tear it up and put it in the front of my underpants and when I'm in the restroom, not even sure if I have real privacy in my stall, flush it all away. I bring this up to my therapist, saying that my GPA is in jeopardy, but they just use it as another excuse to label me as having poor priorities and being even more out of my mind. Apparently, I have more important things to worry about since I'm "in crisis." All of the times jumble together because my parents have requested that I be put on: "the highest doses" of whatever I've been diagnosed with most recently, adding pills upon pills. Usually, it's an argument where I raise my voice and am defiant, not obeying my dad's orders, or maybe a sibling and I get into a fight which could be normal sometimes in other families, it's not like I start them most of the time, but because of my reputation in my family, no matter who started it, who hit who, I know where the fault goes. I also break things sometimes, not knowing how to channel my anger. It's usually not on purpose. Like if I kick and a wall gets a hole in it — it's not like I was trying to, the anger coursed through me. There are other times like that when my body almost involuntarily made a motion, not to anyone, but to an object like a wall or door and it caved to the force, which would scare me sometimes too. But I could never imagine keeping all the sound inside my throat or movements my body wanted to do inside my body. I think I would implode or something. I'm not treated well, but I know it doesn't justify what I do, like an experiment behind plexiglass: how will she react with this cocktail in her system? Will she be tired but able to do her homework? Fine. Is everything at home really magically better when I'm gone? I wonder, and part of me thinks it isn't, then another believes it must be a lot better without me, or why would they keep getting rid of me? Back to the present...

The happiest guy here has big, frizzy/dreadlocked hair and pale skin with a lanky build. He is sitting here in a relaxed posture, smiling, when I sit near him at social hour, and say nothing.

"Hi," he says in a kind, calm tone.

"Hi," I utter as I look up quickly... "What brings you here?" I ask. It's like the "What do you do?" of networking. Cliched, but something people typically have a ready response to. Nothing creative. Easy. Mindless.

His calm demeanor stiffens as he huffs softly, "Weed, man. Just smoking a fucking joint. I'm just glad they didn't find the baggie I hid in my car. I was nervous they'd find it. I would be fucked. It would have been a felony." Our eyes meet and he calms again. "One day this is gonna be legal and all this time will have just been a waste. They'll have to find other ways to occupy their time besides picking up kids just trying to relax. But on the plus side, I have a place to stay for a while now. It's like a vacation from real life."

"Interesting way to think about it." And I let the conversation die.

He doesn't ask me why I'm in, and I feel so glad. I wouldn't have answered, anyway. It's like clockwork, roll in here for a week or several, every few months. For reasons that jumble together; if you asked I couldn't even tell you why, but there are key themes.

It's not what most people would expect. I know that most people can't imagine me as violent, just a quiet, skinny, young, white girl with stringy long hair who looks like the girl from The Ring. But when they (my family) mess with me, hurt me, call me names, it's like the momentum of my emotion multiplies my strength, allowing me to escape most grasps and for an unintentional added effect, break through most literal walls. My dad got in the habit of calling the police as a next step when they felt like I wasn't obeying their authority. He's a police officer rising the ranks, and I can see how one police officer to another, reprimanding their daughter, can be like a professional hand-off. A part of the brotherhood. Some parents ground you for being defiant. Mine call the cops. It's not enough to say "I'm here for being violent," without also adding, "but only at home with my family," and then, "because that's how we communicate. They are violent too, except they don't get in trouble." Too many qualifiers. People get so riled up by the first part that they don't hear the rest, leaving me misunderstood again. People really seem to think that perfectly honest and kind parents can have a demon child. They (my parents) are the victims, and I am this superhuman, angry, wild animal to send away, tranquilize, and fix. My dad always says I need to "stop trying to be the victim" and I feel like I never even tried to and can't think of a time when somebody told me they thought I was. "You're always feeling sorry for yourself," he says, and I think to myself in a silent telepathic reply, "I'm just processing." Wouldn't an emotionally intelligent person think there's more to the story? But people like to simplify things. Have heroes and bad guys, victims and villains. And I have no desire to be a victim.

So, when asked, I usually just sink into my chair or look away, and they get the picture. Anyone can share freely if they want to, and I know my parents have a strong hold on the narrative which paints me as the villain and themselves as the victims. I could defend my reputation with everyone they're telling: teachers, neighbors, their friends, my friends' parents, pretty much everybody, but I choose not to. I want to be known for what is true to me. And if I can't, I'd rather just disappear.

This exchange inspires me to not ask that question anymore.

— —

I am on my period during my pat down in the women's bathroom. The woman doing the pat down asks me to take off my underwear, and then take out my tampon. She knows I'll bleed everywhere, right? And why did nobody need to check here before? Does she think I'm snuggling things inside or some crazy shit like that? Because everyone knows I'm such a druggie (sarcasm) I pull at the string, and drop it on the floor since she hasn't given me permission to move.

"Stand with your legs apart." She stares at me. "Wider," she instructs before walking over, squatting down and inserting a gloved finger into my vagina, feeling along the edges of the inside with more precision than I have at this point in my life.

I wonder if this is normal. I feel my body tense and try to tell myself it's like being at the dentist when they ask you to open up wider, and even if you don't want to, you just do. I hope nobody walks by to see blood dripping down my leg in this open bathroom situation. Is this what it's like at a gynecologist? But she isn't a gynecologist, so probably not.

I feel anger boil up inside of me as my cheeks flush with humiliation. But mostly anger at my parents for putting me here, for this stranger, for putting her fingers inside of me, I feel tears forming and can feel I'm dripping.

After what seems like minutes of her probing around and feeling around and inside, she says, "All right, all clear. Rinse off and put your clothes back on." She throws the worn, yellowing bra and panties at my feet, barely missing the bloody discarded tampon. "Oh yeah, here." She places a pad on top of the pile.

— —

2004, age 14, Novato, CA

"Why are you wearing sweatpants? It's such a hot day!" one of my P.E. mates says during class. There are what they call Indian summers here, so even though it's October, it feels like the hottest part of the year.

I stare back blankly. I'm kind of known for that these days. I don't want them to know the truth and I also don't want to lie. I'm not ignoring the question, per se, but I don't have an audible answer. It's just the way it is. So, these questions get to be met with silence.

It's summer, but I can't wear shorts or everyone at school will see my ankle bracelet. It's how they (my parole officer) can track me and make sure I only go to school and home. Even though the bad stuff only ever happens at home. I know people talk, as in gossip, and I won't be one of them, or contribute to it. I have bigger fish to fry. The first evening I'm home, and wearing it at the dinner table, an episode of the Simpsons airs in which Homer is wearing a tracking bracelet too, and the family laughs in a way that's only slightly strained.

— —

All I'd have to do is go to a friend's house, and I'd be fucked. They're not allowed to visit when I'm home on house arrest either. The thing is, the whole reason I'm on house arrest in my parent's house is because of what's happened in the home. In 'my' home.

"Once you get in the system, it's hard to get out," Ulysses, my probation officer says as he checks on my ankle to make sure the bracelet is still there, where it's court ordered to stay for at least 30 days. He's not lying.

"What kind of one-size-fits all fuckery is this?" I ask, but in more eloquent terms.

"It's the way it is," he offers sternly, and I know better than to probe a probation officer.

This is life. I spend most of my time in my room switching off between listening to music and crying. Sometimes both at the same time. I count down the days until my ankle will be free and look forward to wearing shorts outside. Other times I journal to explain what I'm feeling. It feels like my thoughts are in a cloud from the drugs. Prescription. Some people do drugs for fun, but in my experience, years of being forced to take them,

I've learned there's nothing fun with being so dissociated, forgetting things and feeling tired, except for maybe the numbness. But even that isn't fun, it's just nothing, which is nicer than the alternative sometimes. I get to escape some of my thoughts and feelings and it's closer to not existing. I wouldn't kill myself, but if somebody wanted to, I don't think I'd put up much of a fight right now. There's a hollowness to this existence that I dissolve into sometimes.

I have a feeling the worst part of my life is happening now. If I can just hang in there, it can be more than okay someday. It's a risk I'm willing to take. To stay alive just to see without getting my hopes up.

I decide to call and invite Linda over when nobody's home. I've been in my room barely leaving and haven't seen anyone in a few days, so they (my family) should feel less compelled to call the cops if they do come home and spot her, but I don't intend to let that happen to find out how generous they're feeling. The most crucial part will be the entry and exit. Luckily, my room is close to the front door. I wish I still had a lock on it, but what I can do is play music, which is usual for me, and sit in front of the door to give her more time to hide if anyone does check on me. I try to see her at lunch at school, but can't have a real conversation without privacy. Now that we can, it feels cathartic. We can hug and have 'real talk' about what's happening in this house and in her house. I trust her with my secrets and hope that the secrets stay safe although I'm not really sure they will, just grateful someone is here to listen, but equally grateful to get to hear about her life. What the life of a more normal teenager is like these days... but she assures it's really not that interesting and when I am in school and we hang out at lunch or talk in the locker room before gym, it's all like that, just more often without a break. When I ask about her family, she usually freezes up.

"It's not as bad as you, but..." her voice trails off, but she keeps talking, and I listen.

It's not a contest, but when she compares our families, I know if it was a contest of who has it worse, I'd be winning, and it's a weird idea to consider. I can wear weather- appropriate clothing with my bracelet showing, without fear of judgment, with my friend. There's nothing like liberating the symbol of your lack of freedom with someone you hope you can trust.

I'm not crazy anymore, remember? I'm a criminal. So melodramatic. My parents cannot control me, so they have resorted to calling the police to punish me when I act in a way they don't like, usually once everything is calmed down anyway, even when it's stuff normal kids do.

I can't help but get caught up in the sensationalism of the labels bestowed upon me, but at other moments, let out a giggle at how insane it all is. How insane everyone thinks I am. I oscillate between feeling hopeless and hopeful as often as my parents' reactions to the same things change. I feel a deep hope that as I get older, I will be free to be as perfect or imperfect as I want, and that my best will be enough.

2004, age 14, San Rafael, CA

Before I can go home, I need to go to court. My parents used to be able to take me home once I was discharged from the mental hospital, but in this place, even if my parents want me home sooner, there's nothing they can do. They've given their power away to this place.

I am sitting in the waiting room for those incarcerated, waiting for our hearings. Sitting on a wooden slab littered with graffiti, and I wonder how those people got Sharpies into this room. (Maybe a tampon? Bad joke.)

They don't tell you what time you're going to go. It all depends on how quick the proceedings go, so I could be sitting here all day. Nothing to do but wait. Nobody talks to one another. We may look, silently slouched, looking up at the clock. They don't allow talking while you wait, and I can't imagine what we would even say at a time like this, with so much uncertainty and pent-up nerves mixed with the relief that one way or another, within however many hours' time it takes for them to call your name, you'll know if you're going home today, or not.

Eventually, I'm called into a new room, but it's not the courtroom yet. I have been assigned a public defender with tight gray curls named Margaret. We're about to head into the courtroom and she asks me to talk to her.

"What about anything and everything will be used against me?" I clarify.

"I'm on your side, Stephanie. Feel safe to speak here and I will speak for you out there."

Then I tell her my side of the story, and so many stories... that all the times blur together.

"I make my parents so mad no matter how hard I try to just be neutral. Sometimes they start the fights, sometimes I do. The same thing can be okay one day and make them mad another. Maybe I didn't do the dishes on time or good enough. Maybe I made a mess in the kitchen and didn't clean it up right away. Maybe I disagreed with a sibling and we started yelling. But mostly it would be my attitude, and how I ask "why," about almost everything. Why my parents talk to me and treat me in certain ways. I want to understand it, but I don't think they understand themselves as much as I understand them, or want to. They never get in trouble for it when they start it, it's somehow always "self-defense," but not if I fight back, then I'm being abusive. They are allowed to punish me and have other people punish me, even though their behavior is no example for me to follow with my dad's raised voice, heavy hand, and lack of empathy. They are no better than me, and in my current state, I am no better than them. That last one they tell me all the time, "you think you're so much better than us," like they don't believe it but want me to. Just by being myself, I'm 'wrong' by their unclear rules and when I won't accept it... I end up here. We all get angry for some reason we don't always remember. It could be a comment I made to my dad that was talking back. It could be being chased around the house by my dad, me screaming, trying to get away. It could be like this one time, similar to the reason I'm here today. But this time I was locked out of the house as a punishment after an argument that got heated and I was ready to go back inside. He sat on the other side of the door as though to taunt me. "OPEN. THE DOOR." I instructed with gritted teeth. I know you get further by being nice, but I just can't sometimes. He didn't say anything, walked away, and I lost it. I screamed and banged on the door and I didn't stop until I realized that the screen door had broken from my banging on it. I stopped in my tracks, looked down, ashamed at how I had gotten myself into another one of those situations. I knew I'd be here. Just not this long. Has it been 4 weeks? I think that's a record."

Margaret seems riled up and doesn't quite understand and she looks at me, perplexed. In this instance, I broke something for the first time (if you don't count kicking holes in walls, but that's when I was littler). I explain...

"I was in the front seat parked in the driveway arguing and I kicked my foot up on the windshield and heard a huge crack noise and it was still in one piece, but it now had a crack. Of course I didn't mean to, but they didn't think that. And I did not even feel sorry. It looked like what I feel inside, but they couldn't understand and saw that crack while they can't see or understand me. But then they only feel sorry for themselves."

And then I think Margaret understands and looks a little more deflated.

"So, you did it?"

"Yes, I did. I know that whether it was on purpose or not doesn't matter. I just thought you'd want to know that there was more to the story than me randomly vandalizing my parents' car. I don't want to hurt anything or anyone. Two wrongs don't make a right, but I don't know what else I can do and still have my dignity."

"It's not about dignity right now. It's about getting through it. Even if it means you just stay away from them." Margaret gulps.

"I am in my room almost all the time, but I have to go out for food. I buy my own food with babysitting money, but then Dad gets mad and throws some of it away. It takes up too much space." He thinks I take up too much space.

The door swiftly opens a crack. "The judge is ready for you now," a man in a khaki suit utters before closing the door.

"Okay, we have to leave now, just let me talk for you. I'll do my best here."

"Thank you."

We walk out and see my parents on the other side of the small courtroom. Me versus them, but now it not only feels that way, but looks like it too. Our defenders make statements, and I say that I agree, then when the plaintiff, my parents, representation speaks they also say one word, avoiding eye contact with me. They agree with what he said. You never know if you'll go home or stay longer with one of these hearings, but they only happen every couple of weeks, so if they think you need to be punished longer, then you know you're looking at until the next court day, giving away another one of your days to waiting.

It doesn't matter if they (parents) say they want me home, but they never say that, anyway. It's up to the judge who has the facts. Sometimes I imagine that my parents will be on the other side and against the proper order of things, cut across the room and hug me. It feels exhilarating to think it could happen.

Then say that "We really love her and want her home. We made a mistake by calling the police and can work this out."

And in that moment I feel elated, light, and free. But that isn't what happens. The courts get to decide.

6. MENTAL HOSPITAL

2001 - 2002

"Is the fear worse than the reality, if you got closer?"

-"Villainize" by Stephanie Thoma

2001, age 10, Novato, CA

5150- the police code my dad uses when he calls to have me taken away- he speaks the same language as the cops, since after all, he is a cop too, only in San Francisco instead of Marin. The ultimate version of getting grounded. It's when you're a "danger to yourself or others," and you don't even need to have done anything wrong, they just have to think you could. Sometimes my mom locks the kids in the backroom, not my twin Thomas because we're both ten, but my little sisters Karla who's seven and Cassie who's four... Tyler who is not even one yet, which makes no sense because I am just screaming, not hurting anyone, unless you count their eardrums.

My legs tighten and I lose my breath. They instinctively kick outward, muscles spasming and cramping as I feel my face grow hot. No thoughts. Heart racing. My eyes close and I am engulfed in a dizzying spell of emotion. This feels better than crying. And when the words on the page in my journal just don't fit. When I feel so helpless about my situation. Will it ever get better? Will I ever be free from these labels, these places... When I want them to hear me, see me, understand me, but I get to a place I don't even care anymore. That's when I enter this space. Whether it's hot, warm, cramped and like a personal Hell that I can't escape and all I can do is let a guttural scream escape to temper the internal elements. This is my meditation, I'd later learn.

— —

Mom wants me to wear "peasant blouses" and spend all day shopping, but sometimes we have the same taste in music. Rarely, but it happens. "Drops of Jupiter" by Train is always one song we could sing together in the car. We both get excited whenever it plays and seems to soothe whatever mood is upon us.

When I get upset and scream or kick things, she has started sitting on me now. The therapists say that it's a healthy way to restrain me and keep me from damaging property when I get angry. And all I can think silently to myself is, "Is this how she can feel good about being overweight?" Dad always mentions she's fat, and now it can work in her favor. I don't see how sitting on me so I cannot breathe or move is therapeutic, but it's a new experiment. It always feels like they're using experiments to try to fix me. They want to fix the behavior, but not understand all the reasons behind it.

— —

I'm starting to notice things in the den more. There are lots of books. So many. When I really look at them they align with what I'm learning in school. All about the Nazis. There's Mein Kampf. What's creepy is the collection doesn't seem to just be educational. His dad also has a lot of dead ducks he killed all over his wall in his den. What's up with that? Dad always talks about how proud of a German he is. His dad is 100% German, and I never hear anything about his mom's side. When people say bad things about the Germans and the bad things they did in World War II, it's like something he celebrates. And I don't understand, but know better than to ask. My desire to just stay out of his head is greater than my curiosity.

2001, age 11, Novato, CA

I take a big gulp of air and rush for the door of "my hole" (as in, "go back to your hole before you piss me off more, I don't want to see your face!" it's what my dad calls my room), before my body collapses onto the dark brown carpet, my knees on the floor and my torso draped upon my mattress. My face is hot and damp with tears streaming so much they're nearly audible. Energy is stirring in my stomach like a typhoon and as I open my mouth moments of silence are interspersed with muffled screams as I hold my face to my comforter. My body goes on like this for several minutes before a thought enters my mind.

— —

Auntie Jamie is such an amazing singer, and she encourages me to sing. She usually has a Veronica Lake side part in her medium-long straight golden brown hair, wears slinky dresses when she's performing, knows how to read music and was even on a TV show impersonating Cher with her husband as Sonny and did a really convincing job. I want to be a singer when I grow up. I write songs all the time, sometimes from nothing at all. I could be happy, and a song and their lyrics come to me, and when I'm sad, they really come to me, but I don't always write them down. I don't know if I can really be one, if it's really realistic. I notice adults who say you can be anything you want, all that you can be, but then think, do you really want to be my teacher? Is that what you really wanted when you were a kid?

I haven't met anybody who is really living their dream, but auntie Jamie comes close. She gets paid to go on stages and sing. She encourages me to go for it too. The thing is, I'm not a performer. My parents love it when I learn and sing songs for them at home and a couple of times even at events hosted by their friends in big rooms with maybe fifty people. It's like for a moment all eyes are on me, and not for something bad. It's something people celebrate. It's a show, a performance, but I do my best to let my real self come out. So maybe it doesn't have to be about the performance, it can really be about people enjoying me being right in front of them.

Auntie Jamie says she will drive me to try out for the show Star Search. I can sing and wear anything I want. When we arrive at the auditions, I can see everybody in full makeup and costume. I am very underdressed if we are comparing. There's a blonde girl with a pink tutu and pink cowgirl boots and hot pink lipstick and cheeks with a matching sparkly hat, and a little boy who has a suit on, then me in a tank top and jeans. It's my nicest tank top, though.

They are happy, but in a manic sort of way. I'm in my perpetual sulk from how my life is feeling, but this is an escape from it, a trip to Los Angeles with Auntie Jamie, and that's a lot to be happy about.

I'm placed in a room with three other kids after singing just a line of "Natural Woman", Jamie's favorite song for me to sing.

She wants me to perform it at her wedding soon, so I've been practicing.

The blonde cowgirl goes first, who's maybe nine, sashays across the room and is basically screaming as she's singing, and it's not half bad, she's hitting the notes, but it's more about the performance and jumping around. I think she would sound a lot better if she slowed down, but it's part of her appeal.

When it's my turn, at the last minute I decide to sing Christina Aguilera's "Beautiful," and stand without making any movements, eyes closed. I want to do the song justice, and know I probably shouldn't have changed my song at the last minute but I'm just trying to do what's right. I hardly know what that is sometimes. Then the next guy in the suit who's probably around our age too sings in a sort of whisper but still is walking around the stage.

The judges deliberate, after we are sent to a back room. I devoid myself of emotions. I'm not excited or nervous or anticipating. I realize that everyone else moved around the stage and I didn't, and maybe they won't like that, but I was true to myself, I know I have a good singing voice, and if they really care about my voice and how it can make them money, then maybe they'll pick me, anyway. I don't want to dance though, I just want to sing and not have to pretend or take away from it. I sing when nobody's around more than anything. It's my favorite thing, so while I want to be a singer, I don't know if I can be one because my style is like this. It's not for other people. It's a time that's just for me.

We are called back and the blonde pink cowgirl receives an invitation back to the next step. She excitedly jumps up and down and can't wait for what's next! This is the reaction they want for the camera, which is fine, but not my thing.

Then when it's time for my feedback, they say, "We like your voice, but you need to work on your stage presence. Come back and show more stage presence."

I decide to not come back and say I don't want to do another try out. I have enough to worry about, and I want to be myself more than I want to try to learn how to make people happy on a stage moving around and dancing and smiling when I don't want to.

Auntie Jamie says I did a great job and we go out to eat and I order whatever I want, which I haven't done before. Appetizers and dessert instead of one of those or none. She's so nice. I also know my parents gave her money to spend on me. My dad actually did, because my mom doesn't have money. She gets a weekly allowance from my dad, just like me but more.

My dad also gives her challenges. They are pinned up on the cork board near the calendar on pieces of paper typed and official looking. It's January 1, if she loses twenty pounds before her next birthday in 2 months, she will win

$10,000.000. Dad signs and dates it, and Mom does too, and now it's up for everyone to see. They've done this so many times. Dad really cares about her weight because now that she's overweight he's not as attracted to her. But the thing is, she never completes the challenge.

He says it's simple: "Just stop eating and exercise."

Part of me thinks he offers this to her because he knows he'll never have to pay her out because she won't do it. Doesn't have the willpower, like he does when tasked at something with this much money on the table, but then again maybe her power is in this because he can't control this aspect of her. She eats late at night in the kitchen that's right outside my room. Has secret stashes of chocolates, and on rare occasions she shares her chocolates with me if I am up late like her watching reality tv dating shows. To swap those habits for healthy eating and exercise would take more than a vague intention, but a plan, and she doesn't have one. Also, support, and she doesn't really have that either. I can try to help her make healthy choices. I know it's not my place but I can help her in small ways like walking with her to Sinaloa and back. It's just over a mile.

The sum can even be as much as $25,000, the largest one I saw, with maybe six whole months to do it, and no promise of even keeping it off, and she still signs up for it, and it doesn't happen. I don't think Mom wants these challenges posted publicly for all the kids and their friends coming by to see, but maybe it's part of the deal in order to get the possible reward.

One time I walked in on my mom and dad talking. Mom looked super sad and asked Dad for more money for her allowance, and said "I need to buy tampons, Tom." with a downcast gaze.

Dad could tell I was in the room, I walked in just after she had said this under her breath, and he replied without skipping a beat, "You can just put a sock up there. I'm not giving you any more money."

It's moments like those I know it's none of my business but I lose respect for my mom. Of course she can't stand up for me when she's not even standing up for herself, and part of me pities this and also resents it. Just do something different. Demand instead of asking so nicely when it's something you need. And then I make mental notes that I want to be around men who care about my period when I'm older. It's a scene that reads like a warning.

— —

I wonder if it would be different if I got to stay in school all the time. Would I have friends? Would I know all fifty- states like most others do? My teacher said I didn't have to take the test because I missed the whole section that taught it. People are singing a song and I wish I knew it too.

"It's okay, you have more important things to worry about," the teacher says and I know he's trying to be nice, but I want to know what they are.

— —

We just had a fight, Karla and I. It started with a disagreement, then we hit each other. I know she's 3 years younger than me, and I'm 11 and she's 8, but I still don't think it's wrong. Don't other siblings hit each other and maybe just get a timeout? Why do I have to be sent away instead? Why is she held to a different standard than me? I know I am scary when I'm mad but we hurt each other the same amount. Her nails are longer than mine too.

She is mad at me and my dad says that he's going to try something new. "I won't call the police on you, Stephanie, unless Karla wants me to. You can stay home, unless Karla wants you to be taken away. I support whatever Karla decides. What do you want, Karla?"

Karla looks at me, sitting up on the countertop sitting next to Dad, who's standing. Peering down at me crying on the floor below them. I know better than to plead or get mad. I just watch. Karla puts her little hand on her chin and taps it as she looks at me, with a slight smile emerging on her face. She pauses which looks like it's for dramatic effect, looks up and then to the side and continues tapping on the tip of her chin. "Take her away!" she says pointing her finger up in the air.

I spend the rest of the night in my room and hope they'll forget about me. But what feels like hours later I see the police car from my window. It always goes like this. My dad talks with the officers telling them how deranged I am, using all the code words.

The police officers may come up to me briefly and ask what happened, take a few notes, but nothing I say matters or makes a difference. I'm taken away again that night.

I know better than to think Karla really decided. I am mad at my dad for giving her false power over me. I'm supposed to be the big sister she looks up to. And I'm sad that Karla went along with it. That she doesn't look up to me, except for sometimes when I sing.

Then if I'm going to the hospital, they'll call an ambulance where I have to be strapped onto a gurney, spending the 30-minute drive with an EMT talking with me, saying nice things, but I don't let it in. I just try to imagine I am not there. And then the whole intake process of either going straight to the hospital, or a holding center where they figure out if they are going to bring me there or somewhere else. Depending on my dad's account of events, they sometimes question where to have me go. I usually keep my cool, but there was a time I was so hungry, it was about 1am and they had me in limbo since about 9pm when I was newly 11, that I screamed, "get me out of here!" and they ended up strapping me to the gurney again and threatening me with an injection with a thick needle to put me to sleep for a few hours if I didn't stop. I only like butterfly needles, that one is too big, I rationalized, so I became quiet and tried to fall asleep on my own.

— —

We are at home one time when my mom calls the police. She has been getting more physical with me when I make bitchy comments, since my dad recommends it will be how I gain respect for her — if she starts to be rougher with me. She's desperate and I hear her agree to try this one day. I don't think they both realize that I actually lose respect for anyone who hurts me. They don't ask. I'm waiting in my room like I usually do on a hot summer day, sometimes the reasons actually make me angrier, like when it's really hot out. This officer asks to meet with me privately, which most cops don't do. We go into the kitchen area and he sits on the bench of the long table where we have our family dinners, and I sit right on the table's top.

"Hey, how are you?" His name is like my dad's, but spelled differently. He also has a badge like his.

I am silent and planning to not say a word (anything- and-everything-you-say-can-and-will-be-used-against-you) but the way he puts his hand on my shoulder and looks at me and waits for me to answer feels different.

Tears stream down my face like a faucet as my eyes meet his and I utter, "Not good..."

"Let the tears come out. Can I hug you?"

"Yes," I say and cry harder into his shoulder, snot, and muffled sounds as he pats me on the back. A few moments later, I pull away.

"It feels like you don't really fit in here, doesn't it? Like Mom and Dad don't understand you?"

Uh-huh, I shake my head up and down. Confused. When is he putting the handcuffs on me?

"Do you want to tell me your side of what happened?"

And I do. He sits with me and listens, and I talk about everything that happened and how both of my parents say "I hate you" more than "I love you," and push me around and I push back, and they ask my siblings in front of me to "pick a side" theirs or mine, when I really just want to be a part of the family and have all of us on one side... and of course they don't pick my side... the feelings I felt and he doesn't tell me that I'm wrong.

"I believe you," he says without skipping a beat. "Now my question for you is, do you feel safe here, or do you want to come with me?"

I've never had the option before. I choose the only option that contrasts what usually happens. "I want to stay."

"If that's really what you want, you can."

"Yes, I want to stay," I say, viscerally feeling the power of this moment. I don't know if I really want to, but I wonder... Was it always really up to my mom or dad whether I went away or not? Or do these officers get to decide?

"Yeah, I feel bad for him, he's so small," my roommate says to me as we stand in our doorway looking across the hallway at him crying in his doorway. Singing. Sobbing. In the way crazy homeless people, or toddlers, do.

"He's six years old... I didn't know they took anyone that young here," I say, nearly double his age.

"No child should have to be here. Not this young," my roommate says and we hear footsteps coming toward our doors, we scurry back to our beds before the night staff can see us.

I wonder what it would be like if I started that young. I started coming here to the mental hospital when I was ten. Would I be more used to it? Or is it the kind of place you never get used to? The lemon scented sheets. The fluorescent lights that are always on and make everything yellow-tinted during the day and night. The lunches where everything is individually wrapped like you're getting a school lunch. Breakfast and dinners are like that, too. I try to remember back to when I was his age and I just can't. Was I happy and playing outside? Or was I inside wishing I was somewhere else? Maybe a mix of each. I have seen school pictures from those years where I couldn't smile. Or where my mouth is happy but my eyes are still sad. When I was six, I must have been singing and sobbing like him, too.

2002, age 11, Novato, CA

I walked in on him butchering one of the family sheep in the barn — a total surprise and shock. Sally. He planted her head in the backyard. Her eyes were still open. He served her to us for dinner and I left the table.

"I only care if it's my blood," he says about things like that.

The pain of others.

2002, age 11, Vallejo, CA

Jewel always understood me in ways most people didn't. When I was little, she called me "Princess Monster Stephanie" because we loved playing "Pretty, Pretty Princess," the board game with jewelry you can wear, but sometimes my monster side would come out, she said. I could be happy and fine and then filled with rage. She always knew it was something deeper, but she told me not everybody would know that. And I told her not everybody sees this side. I can only show it to family, I decided. Even if they don't want it. I wish she would just call me Princess Stephanie. But she's always there when I call her and she writes me letters and tells me life will get better for me. When I think to myself, sometimes I hear her voice, telling me that over and over at night.

She visited me in the mental hospital more than once when I was ten and eleven and twelve, probably at least once a year. Bringing magazines in with her at times. Once there was one with Britney Spears on the cover. I had sung one of her songs in the talent show a few years earlier. "She looks so pretty, but why are her cheeks so much darker than her forehead?"

"It's retouching. Makeup. She doesn't really look like that. If she did, she would look silly. You don't need to look like that, Steph."

2002, age 12 Vallejo, CA

I start crying in the middle of the night. The tears stream down my face like a river, and then the sound comes out. A slight moan. Then it's fuller. And before I know it I'm screaming.

Someone from the front desk rushes in, concerned about me waking everyone up.

"Hey, are you okay? Can you tell me what's wrong?"

My screams get louder. Not out of defiance, but because I don't know what to do with this question. I don't know what's wrong, and it makes me angry. My body shakes with how angry I am.

Within minutes she gets another employee to carry me to a room. It's padded. I'd usually been so good and didn't think I'd end up here, but here we are. There's a first time for everything. When they pick me up I instinctively kick and wail my body to escape their grasp. They call for backup. They need "all hands on deck." I'm in the padded room, and it's also soundproofed. They strap me down on a cold table and rip my pants and underwear down- a staple of my usual punishments. I'm facing the opposite of the door, but pull my face up to see another person enter the room with a large needle. This is new to me.

"Stop moving," The first woman who entered the room whispers. She repeats that in my ear, and I take it as a challenge.

"Stop! No!" I wail on repeat, trying to free myself before I feel it enter me bluntly.

The next thing I remember, I wake up, maybe it's been an hour, or a few. It doesn't seem like it's breakfast yet. "I have to use the bathroom," I call out. Typically, I would tiptoe past my roommate and stand at my door in the illuminated hallway and wait for a staff member to give me permission to make the short walk down the hall.

"I have to use the bathroom!" I yell again, realizing that nobody can hear me, and I cry out more, "I have to use the bathroom! I really have to go! Please let me go!" and realize nobody is coming. Has anybody checked on me? Can I wait long enough until the next time they do, if they do?

The more I cry, it gets harder to hold it in. I feel the warmth gliding down my leg, settling in a puddle underneath my thighs. A contrast to the dull burning sensation I can still feel from the shot in my butt. I'm eleven. I haven't peed myself in so many years, but I didn't have a choice. Maybe if I just calmed down I could have kept it from happening. But it happened, and I feel relieved and wet and disgusted and disgusting and just want to retreat back to sleep and forget this ever happened.

My auntie Jamie got married over the weekend. I was supposed to be singing at her wedding and did my best to be on my best behavior so I could go, and not be sent here at the mental hospital. I was at the rehearsal and it was all so beautiful I couldn't imagine being there on the even more beautiful real day. Maybe I jinxed it. She picked out a beautiful silky lilac dress for me with spaghetti straps, and I was going to wear my light pink butterfly hair clips, but I was bad again, and I couldn't go. Auntie Jamie sings for a living, and I learned a song just for her. "Natural Woman." I hope that she isn't sad and knows that I did my best and can forgive me.

Maybe that's why I woke up crying.

— —

A woman with a clipboard is speaking to me in the common area of the mental hospital where we just had a communal breakfast, but everyone else has gone off to school and now she is here talking with me. She says I can trust her. She has a low brunette ponytail and a mole under her left eye, and a clipboard. She obviously wants me to trust her and I obviously have no intention to. She's a case manager at the hospital and this actually feels less routine, like she might be on my side, but I can't tell and better safe than sorry.

"How did you get that scratch on your face?" "I don't want to talk about it."

"You know, you can tell me," she says softly.

"Yeah, but you'll tell people. And even though I don't like being there, I also don't like being here. If I tell you what happened, I'm afraid I'll be taken away."

"Where is there? Where will you be taken away from?" "Home."

We sit in silence for several minutes. She must know that I could stay this way for hours. Tight-lipped and fine with it.

She breaks the silence. "We talked with your mom and she said that her ring accidentally got to your face. She says that it was self-defense."

I can feel my face engorge with blood and my legs coursing with tension, and I'm silent. I thought we would look out for each other in what I realize was an optimistic delusion. I wouldn't say it was her fault and then I could go home. I never imagined she'd lie.

Here's what happened: My mom and I were arguing as usual (Does it even matter what the topic was? Rarely). I made a "smartass" remark which some would probably call witty, and she looked at me with narrow eyes and stood up, initiating what happened next.

"You want to fight? That's what you want, you little fucking bitch? Let's go! Fuck you, bitch!" she said with her hands in fists and her voice loud but cracking and eyes partially closed.

"Go fuck yourself. You're not scared that I would beat you? Stop trying to be like Dad," I snapped.

"I'm not trying to be like Dad... bitch," she said under her breath with a lower register force, with an undercurrent of adrenaline and nerves, like this was her chance to prove her power over me.

I stood up and who even knows who starts, but our fists were swinging. I hadn't fought like this before, with the formality of a duel but much closer and more personal. Usually, I'm chased first. I can tell she's not hitting me as hard as she can, but she's stronger, so maybe that makes it fair. With my shoves, I can see her getting dizzy and being thrown off balance — my goal is to knock her down and I really don't care if she gets roughed up in the process. She usually just watches me get hurt and now she wants to fight? Let her see how it feels. She lets out whimpers and grunts with every swing, and at one point I feel a hot slice across my cheek.

"Oh my god..." she says. "You know I didn't mean that," she yells.

"What the fuck Mom! Fuck you!" I held my face with blood on my hand.

"Fuck you! You just have to go. This is out of control." She scurries to the phone and I know who she's calling. I know what's happening. And my heart drops and it's like a train coming on schedule- I anticipated it but also wished for it to not come. This pattern of reality was stronger than the wish.

"They're coming. Let me get you some Neosporin. You know I didn't mean that, right?"

And I don't answer even though I hear her since I'm already in my room. The place I always retreat to when the calls are made. A place where I can be alone and sometimes hear, other times not hear what they say about me to solidify my fate for weeks to come.

And then the cops come and talk to my mom before an ambulance comes and they take me away. Now I'm in this room at the hospital with this stranger who's telling me Mom's story. They (staff members) haven't believed me before, and my mom already told her side. If everyone thinks it was a total accident, I get to stay home and I won't have to worry about never getting to come home again. I love my little brother Tyler, he is so cute. He's almost two. And I can tell he loves me, too. I just get to hold him and change his diapers and play with him and he doesn't know any better but to love me right back. I don't know how long that will last. And what if it's even worse getting sent away?

"I don't think she meant it," I confirm, and stay silent about the rest, a strategic choice.

Then I have to stay there overnight and I wonder what it could have been like if I told my side and they believed me.

We'd drive for over an hour because I qualified. Stanford is paying parents to study the brains of mentally ill children, and according to the diagnoses based on my parents' accounts and therapist meetings I refused to speak in, I fit the bill for being fit for a variety of paid case studies: bipolar disorder, OCD, borderline personality disorder, chronic depression, generalized anxiety disorder, the list is as long as the medications I am forced to take.

The CAT scan machines sound like a computer turning on, dialing up, and I have to look at dots of light and click when I see them, or watch movies and say if I feel sad.

One time we are waiting for two hours and the researcher never comes. Turns out she was running around the track and hit her head and wasn't well enough to conduct the scans so I needed to come back extra times. I remember sitting in on the results one time when my mom was getting the check. They said the scan seemed normal, which seemed to disappoint her. This was for bipolar disorder. I probably had something else then, my mom rationalized, but I felt a little bit happy about it, maybe I'm *actually* okay.

I routinely miss the same classes with this new study I am a part of, so I spend the mornings in the Stanford waiting rooms getting ahead on my other classes, reading chapters that aren't assigned, or double-checking my homework. This is what I need to do to try to maintain my work ethic and a chance at getting a good GPA. The school officials say I can revisit after a semester and possibly take the classes over, but my intention is to stay on track and not fall behind. Once the semester is over, I am released from the study to have a better chance at attending regular classes at school.

I remember being in IEP meetings. The money the grant participants receive is intended to go toward my growth and development, since I'm an "at risk youth" and "mentally unwell," but I don't want anything. They are mostly talking about getting money and how my parents are low income, but I don't think we actually are. Instead of accepting my answer, I don't want anything, it turns into an opportunity for my siblings to get things. My mom says the family needs money for my brother's sports cleats or something. I always zone out during the meetings. Why can't Mom and Dad pay for their own stuff? Why do they need me to be in this program to benefit the other kids? Why aren't the other kids eligible?

Maybe this is their way to try to get paid back for all of the money they have been spending to prove their hypothesis right- that I am messed up and they are not.

— —

One day my parents are meeting with my 6th grade teacher and I am waiting in another classroom by myself for what felt like hours. He is a quirky guy who cracks jokes that make me smile sometimes. He likes my writing and usually gives me good grades for my work. As I am doing my homework, my 6th grade teacher burst through the door, red faced and catching his breath. "You are a good kid," he says to me, or the room itself. He gets slightly closer and lowers his tone, looks me in the eye, exasperated, and says, "No matter what they say, I want you to know you're a good kid, okay?" and I take a breath and gulp, "okay."

I get assigned another free service- a YMCA mentor. She often pays me to babysit, including watching her two-year- old during her 30th birthday party, and I feel a sense of trust with Ali. She is so pretty, blonde and into health and we pick figs from her backyard and she makes parfaits with yogurt and granola- I'd never had those and they tasted so good! No added sugar too, which she says is important. I thought only candy had a lot of sugar. We meet at her yellow house only a couple of miles from me weekly and I watch how she speaks with her husband, the way she dresses too. I like her. It seems like she must have been popular in school which I could not relate to, but we connect on other levels. She is curious about my life, not what is wrong, but what my goals are and what I like to do. She is a light in my life.

— —

Whenever I have holes in my pants and want to sew it, I ask Dad. Although I could do it myself, there's something about the way he does it. He never seems happy when I ask him, "Dad can you sew a pair of my pants?" usually at the crotch, but it saves him money on new pants and makes him feel needed so maybe that's why he says "Yes."

Sometimes I'll walk by and see the concerted dedication of him trying to match the thread with the inseam color of my pants, holding it up to his face so he gets it as 'right' as he can, with a sweet concentration. This lets me know maybe he loves me, and I let the gratitude linger whenever I return to the laundry room and see he's folded the newly mended pants and left them on top of the washing machine for me.

7. ORIGINS

1991 - 2000

"She has a temper, you know, she'll scratch your eyes out, you know, be afraid and leave her by herself."

- "Villainize" by Stephanie Thoma

1991, age 2, San Francisco, CA

My parents tell me that as a baby I had colic, and was usually up all night crying. It's when you have gas and can barely move with discomfort gastro-intestinally. They say I'd also stay awake for my dad during his night shift. I'd will my eyes to stay open and close them once he gave me a kiss on the forehead. A sort of permission.

1994, age 4, Novato, CA

I look up at Thomas' big horsey toy. Mom and Dad have never gotten me anything so big. I wonder if that means they love him more. I asked about it and they said that Thomas will share it and I can use it when I want to. I don't have much interest in it, preferring one of those pink cars I could drive around in but Dad says we can't afford. One day I get on the horsey. Thomas sees this and gets angry. I wonder if he knows that I am allowed to do this. He proceeds to walk up to the horse and pull me off and repeatedly hit me. There's a split second where I am about to fight back, but I look up and see my dad. He will save me. My body goes limp so he can come over and pick me up out of this and hug me and put me back on the horse. Instead, I see my dad laughing and feel the deepest sadness I can remember. My entire body stays limp and I cry not because of the hits, but at the laughter.

"Go get her, Thomas!" he cheers, and I realize he's not on my team.

Maybe if I was winning, but I'm not. I'm too distraught to try to be a winner for him or myself. Whatever happened to my body pales in comparison to the pain of loss in those moments.

— —

I remember going to ice cream shops and being on Daddy's shoulders.

"Daddy, uppy!" I'd exclaim and he'd swoop me up and I'd hold on, but he was already holding onto my knees so I wouldn't fall off. He would always take a big lick of my ice cream cone so it wouldn't drip all over. He had to get it ready first. Then I got to have it as my own, and it wouldn't make any mess. I was always a bit more focused on him being happy than how I felt, so those times were great. Those were some of the sweetest times I can remember.

1995, age 4, Novato, CA

We have a weekly burrito night where Dad gets toppings together, and it's usually on Tuesdays. He makes ground beef, shredded cheddar, black olives, lettuce, tomatoes and maybe vegetables and we all sit around the table to watch something like the Simpsons or that cartoon with the dinosaurs. It feels like it's TV meant for kids and adults, or maybe more adults but it's cartoon so kind of the same. On Fridays Dad makes lasagna that's always a bit burnt on the top and I learn to prefer it like that. "I want the crispy piece" all of us say in unison, and if I am on my dad's good side I might get it if I wait for permission, or if I take it upon myself to grab the first-choice piece. I used to have a seat very close to him, but one year I can't remember if it was me or him, but now I'm as far away as you can be at the table. Mom and Dad want us to prioritize eating as a family regularly, like they never had. It's a tradition and the food is better than what they normally feed us, like banquet TV dinners when they are on sale for one dollar or fried bologna sandwiches.

— —

My hot pink Barbie lunchbox has glitter on the sides. When it's lunch time I open my lunchbox to find there's a note that says *I love you* with a heart, and gummy bears and a sandwich and carefully wrapped snacks, and it seems so different, but I like it. I feel amused and loved and begin to eat the strange food, and savor the note.

Across the room another girl is crying, "I didn't get my love note... ewww what is this?" She's holding up a sandwich like the one my dad usually makes me with bologna and mustard. I realize mid-bite that we have the same lunchbox and I am actually eating her lunch. I take a moment to let this sink in, cutting off emotions before they can surface, *Of course it belongs to her, getting it back will make her happy while I get what I would have expected*, I rationalize, before walking up to her to exchange it back, and then she looks excited and reads her note and stops crying.

1995, age 5, Novato, CA

Dad says when he was dating before he met Mom, some of them thought they were all that and a bag of chips. He said his grandpa had a phrase about women like that. "You think you're hot snot but you're cold boogers."

1996, age 5, Novato, CA

There's a picture in the living room of Thomas and I at the park when we were toddlers.

We're wearing Sesame Street sweatshirts and I'm standing proudly holding a stick and Thomas is crying. My parents recount that I had stuck up for him when the geese started walking toward him, waddling in a herd, attempting to nip him with their beaks. As they drew closer, surrounding him, Thomas crying on the ground almost resigned to his fate, I grabbed a stick and charged at them, chasing them, and yelling as I swung the stick in the air.

— —

I apparently would watch my blood being drawn. Dad liked this. He always wanted a tough son, he said, but he got a tough daughter instead. I wonder if I am actually that tough. I never thought of myself that way. Am I allowed to be not tough? What about when I don't feel brave, what happens then?

1997, age 6, Novato, CA

Dad takes me fishing all the time. It doesn't even seem like it's about catching fish, he just likes to sit in silence with me, and since that's what he likes, I like it too. He teaches me how to put worms or other bait on the hook, and how to wait as long as it takes until you can't wait anymore or it gets dark and you have to go home. He said if I caught a fish we could eat it.

One day, after hours of waiting as usual, I feel a tug on my pink Barbie branded reel. I just about lose it. "Daddy! Daddy! I got a fish!" I exclaim, as though this is quite possibly the highlight of my life.

"Let's see what you have here," he says with a light smile and gentle grasp of my reel.

When we reel it up and it comes up above the water, he starts to giggle slightly, "It's a goldfish."

"Yeah, it is Dad, but we're going to eat it," I say, knowing it's probably only enough for one baby bite.

"No, Stephanie, we're going to let it go. You have to let it go back to its mommy."

"But I still want to eat it." But after looking at it, I agree it should go back with its family.

Then we sit back down, and within a few more hours, don't catch anything else, and go home.

1997, age 7, Novato, CA

At the end of the year, we get our yearbook, and it asks "One memory I will never forget is when..." and I finish it without hesitation, "when I was suspended from school for one week." Here's what happened.

I'm on the playground and see my friend Shannon playing tag. She's playing with older boys. They're nine.

She runs up to me. "Stephanie, I'm so tired, but they won't stop chasing me! I'm afraid they'll tackle me."

I start jogging with them all and shout back, "Hey guys, stop chasing her, she's done!"

"No, she's not!" one asserts, and another chimes in, "Okay, we'll start chasing you!"

I run for a little while before I decide that I don't want to play. I never wanted to.

While I slow my jog, I shout back, "I'm done, guys. You can play with someone else who wants to play."

"No, you're not!" one of them shouts.

Once I stop, one of the guys trips me and tackles me to the ground on the blacktop concrete. He's on top of me, pulling at my clothes and shoving his hands on my skin in a rough way that reminds me of getting rug burn, and in a moment I go limp, calculating what to do next, and then use all of my strength to shove up and down, and now I am on top of him. I am straddling his torso and mercilessly kicking his legs under mine and hitting his head and arms and chest and through the momentum see his surprise as he is screaming, "Stop! Stop! Helppppp! Heeeeeelp!"

A yard duty looks over and I don't stop until after she's all the way here.

"What's going on here?" she asks.

"She just started hitting me and tackling me," he says through muffled tears.

"He tackled me first. You only saw the second part." I say matter-of-factly.

We go to the principal's office separately. There's also his friend as a witness to it all who is of course biased, and the yard duty who only saw my part. My friend is playing a new game by that time and doesn't see this unfolding. I am deemed at fault and am suspended from school for a week. When my parents have to pick me up early from school that day, they seem confused at first. I'm never violent at school. I tell them what happened, and that I was defending myself.

They say they believe me and take me out for ice cream.

My mom and dad say they are proud of me.

"You should always stand up for yourself," Dad says. "That's my girl," my mom says as she shares how she

used to get beat up at school for no reason as a kid. It's like she feels this hollow victory as a vindication of her own experience.

And I can tell my mom gets an extra kick out of the fact that the nine-year-old boy was in worse shape than me.

I don't let the appreciation seep in too much. I just know I did what I felt was right at the time. Standing up for a friend. Then, taking extra care to ensure those boys would think twice about chasing and tackling people who don't want it. And sometimes people agree with your actions and other times people don't.

It wasn't until I thought about it later that I felt guilty- for continuing to hurt him after he said "Stop," like all the times I said, "Stop." But just as quickly rationalized, it's not my fault they came after me and underestimated my strength. Now they know.

— —

I am in my room and so is Dad. Sometimes when I run and shut the door, it'll be over. Other times, it is only the beginning. Recalling one of the stories my dad had told me, he said George Washington cut down a cherry tree. "Never shall I tell a lie, father, I did it," was what George had said to his dad when asked what happened. George wasn't beaten because his dad appreciated hearing the truth. Another time, my dad shared a personal story. He anticipated getting 'a beating' from a teacher and put a book in his pants so when she spanked him, he didn't really feel it.

I recite the line he taught me to lighten the mood and maybe he'll like that I remember what he said. "Never shall I tell a lie father, I did it," stoically escapes my lips when he asks if I had done the thing he thought I did, and moments later he's in a rage, and it hurts. I usually don't remember what I did wrong as much as the punishment. If he explained why what I did was a bad choice, instead of saying that I'm bad, then maybe I'd learn something.

This isn't how the story goes. I think. He's supposed to like that I internalized the message he taught me. Maybe he doesn't value honesty after all. Maybe it was a story that he liked to tell, but it was nothing more than that. How another family dealt with things. Maybe it was just a stupid story.

— —

I place books in my pants in preparation for spanking. I don't remember what I did, but by Dad's reaction, he's mad: his face is red, the vein in his neck is getting bigger, his voice gets deeper and he's ready to run after me... it's going to happen. A day I leave "my hole" is likely a day I get spanked. I will inevitably say the wrong thing, ask for something unwarranted, have a tantrum when I feel unheard, or challenge a way of being that has no desire to change.

In my room he starts spanking as usual, before saying, "What's this?"

"Books," I say with a slight smile, hoping he'll snap out of it and be endeared. I did what he did.

Instead, he's livid and rips the books out from my underwear, and hits me even harder.

"Why are you doing this to me?" I sob, and repeat the phrase over and over until I can't articulate words anymore. As I become tired and numb, I can feel him calm down.

He reaches down and whispers, "It's okay. Shh. It's okay," as he cradles my limp chest and I feel the contrast of love from hate. He would be indifferent if he didn't care, right? This part of him that's gentle with me fills my heart, contrasting the pain, amplified by it. I feel sore and delighted and confused. He kisses me on the forehead before he leaves and I cry myself to sleep.

NOT THAT SWEET

— —

One day, Dad finds my journal. He's been in my room. It is my favorite one because it looks like a real book with a big spine and 3D decal on the front. My Grandma Judith got it for me- it's sparkly dark green with a decal of ruby red slippers like the ones I have on it and a yellow brick road. It says *There's No Place Like Home* on the cover and I put another sticker I got in a magazine below that reads *Stay Out!*

He is mad and holding it and he's ripped it in half. He's yelling, but I don't understand most of the words, they're so fast.

My mom stands to the side, keeping her distance, and says, "Tom, calm down. Don't do this. Tom," but he can't hear her.

"You want her to be able to keep this absolute garbage? Look at this, she writes, "I hate my brother Thomas," and draws a picture of him picking his nose. Jean, this isn't okay! Fucking bullshit!"

"Tom..." and her voice trails off and she looks away.

"Okay, come here." He looks at me and takes a step toward me, and I bolt down the hallway into my room.

I want my journal back but not that badly. But now when I rush into my room, I don't have it to write in. This is the loneliest. Why am I not allowed to do what they do? Why can't I be mad and write words and draw pictures that show that? It wasn't for them to see, anyway. My mom seemed to think he was overreacting, too. She comes in probably a few hours later and hands me the book and we find some tape, and don't talk about it.

I am supposed to be singing in a school choir, an array of old-time holiday songs. Dad walks me over to the classroom in my holiday dress one night after school is over. All of the other kids are with a parent or two, and it just seemed different. They seem happy. Before I go inside, Dad whispers something to me, "You better sing, drop the pouty shit, then right when you're done, we're out of here," and even though I love to sing, I don't feel like it. Even though I am on stage and everyone else is smiling, I don't feel like it. So, I stand there, mouth closed, trying not to cry or look at my dad. I'm not in the holiday spirit. I just want to go home. I was excited, but not anymore.

When the performance is over, my dad quickly runs over to me, grabs my arm, and pulls me outside. Many people are still hanging out and mingling with other moms and dads and kids in the classroom, but my dad has another plan.

He yanks me onto the bench in front of the classroom and rips down my white tights and underwear, and starts slapping my bare bottom. "You ungrateful little... you embarrassed me in there. All you had to do was sing. I can't believe I drove us all the way here so you could humiliate me. You were looking all pouty up there, and the only one! Let's give you something to cry about."

We are right next to the door. I hear one mom gasp, and the rest seem quiet and I hear them hurriedly step away, or make comments to their kids like, "Aren't you excited for dinner tonight?"

I feel like I'm on display, but nobody wants to see this. Like I could have avoided all of this if I just put on a smile and sang.

If I ran off the stage before it started and told him I couldn't do it, I think the same thing would have happened. The only correct option was to perform, but that didn't feel like an option I wanted to entertain, even if it was the easiest.

At least we are on holiday break and I don't have to see anyone tomorrow. Hopefully they'll forget when we go back to school next year.

— —

I write in my journal every day. I don't understand why some people think reading is easier or better. When there's so much going on in your own life, in your own head and with your own feelings. My favorite thing to do is write. I go through at least one journal a year. It listens to me and understands me. I can feel bad for myself and also tell myself that it's okay, then read it back, and it's like it's saying it to me. I don't know why my parents hate me so much. It's not fair that they decided to give birth to me but don't want me. Then why did you make me exist? They talk about giving me away and getting rid of me all of the time.

"You have to earn your keep," Dad always says about chores like the dishes, and rubbing his feet, and doing whatever he says, "Because I said so."

But I'm also curious about a better reason. But why do I have to earn it if I don't even want it? Why can't I be here and have that be enough? If I didn't choose to be born, can't they just be happy I'm here without me needing to prove they made the right choice to have me? Even on the days I do everything I am told, I feel just as empty as when I don't, just more empty, less alive. They say "I hate you," to me more than "I love you," and

I say it too, louder than they do, though. Sometimes I cry in the mirror and think about that girl that I see. I look straight in her eyes and see how sad she is, and I whisper, "You are going to get through this. Life is going to be really good one day. Auntie Jewel loves you, and I do too. I would hug you if I could. One day, it will be better. I love you so much." And I believe her.

— —

When Dad's drunk, he says a lot of things. Things I don't know how to respond to, like "If you weren't my daughter, I'd date you." or "Don't ever change... you're at the perfect weight." "If you wanted to be a Playboy model, you could. I think you have every right to do that."

It just feels creepy. But I knew what he means. He is complimenting me. He is trying to be nice.

When I tell Mom, she just says, "Don't listen to your father..."

1998, age 7, Novato, CA

We go to Sunday school each week, and it's not clear why. All the other kids there, some who even go to my elementary school, also go, but they read the bible for fun at home. We don't read the bible at my house. Their parents are also attending church while we are in Sunday school. But my parents drop us off and leave, my twin brother, me, Karla, and Cassie, who goes to the baby daycare. They talk about stories from the bible like they're things we all know and I feel like I have to tell the teacher after class, "Hey, we don't know any of these stories- the only time we spend with the bible is when we are at Sunday school, so I feel confused when you share certain stories from it."

The teachers just smile after looking a little bit confused and tell me it's okay and they hope I'll continue to join them. That I am welcome here. I'm sure they would give me a bible if I wanted one, but I don't. After a few weeks of this, I am only really looking forward to the donuts that we get to eat, but that's only at the very beginning or very end of class, so after class one day when my other siblings aren't around, I ask my dad. "Why do we go to Sunday school?"

"It's good for you." "Why?"

"Because I said so."

"I don't want to go. And you and Mom don't even go to church like the other moms and dads."

"This isn't your choice right now," he says, irritably. "When will it be my choice?" I inquire calmly. "When you're ten."

"Okay Dad, so in three years I can decide?" "Yes."

And in three more years, I no longer have to go to Sunday School, and my siblings get to decide too even though they are younger than ten.

1998, age 8, Novato, CA

The new Britney Spears album is always played during free-time and the girls are making up dance moves to it, the boys have Legos, and I am in the corner writing. Mr. Beaver asked me to stay after class. He's wearing a fleece pullover, just like me. His is dark forest green and brown, and mine is bright pink, lime green and orange in a similar zig-zag pattern.

"Can I hug you goodbye?" he asks, and I nod my head "yes," wondering why he didn't hug everybody else. He always asks me to stay later after class to give me a hug, and says he knows things are hard at home and is here if I need him, but this time it's different.

He comes up behind me and says, "You're so special, Stephanie," as he puts his hands over my belly, and then his hands go up to my chest and circle around my tee-tees. "You feel so soft," he says in a long, wispy tone. His voice is deeper than usual. Nobody's ever hugged me like that before, but I quickly decide I don't like it, and move away, several feet away, turn around and just look at him.

"I won't hug you again if you don't want me to," he says calmly.

"I don't like that." I stand two yards away, staring at him in the eyes, body stiff, tone firm, frozen.

"Okay. Have a good day. See you tomorrow."

And then things in class are normal again. He asks me to stay later a few more times in a soft-spoken tone and I just walk by him without acknowledging him. What's he going to do? Call me disobedient and get me in more trouble?

— —

Every now and then, we perform talent shows. It's me as the singer, Karla as my interpretive backup dancer, and Cassie sometimes doing a mix of backup vocals or dance. She is only two, after all. I usually help decide who wears which outfits, and these are the times when I feel like they look up to me. And Mom and Dad and Thomas stop what they're doing, and I sing for them. Sometimes songs I made up, other times Britney Spears songs and I dress up like a princess and feel it's my truth. I'm the happiest when I'm in front of the room wearing a crown, singing with people watching, where nobody can touch me and all I feel is love.

— —

"You know what would cause you to be more tough and independent? Walking to school. You can do it tomorrow morning. I think you can do it. Find your way. You know the turns to take- we've walked it before. Just don't tell your Mom," my dad says.

I nod, a promise. I am eight-years-old and had recently learned of abductions. I think it was on TV, where this little girl was going to school as she normally did and didn't come home. She was eleven-years-old, even older, and bigger than me. They found her again as an adult and she's (understandably) screwy right now, getting back to normal. I wonder why Dad wants me to walk, but is driving Thomas to school.

When I ask, Dad says "Thomas doesn't need to do this. He's not tough enough, anyway. It's like an adventure. When I was a kid, they dropped us all off far away and we had to find our way back," he says wistfully looking up as though lost in a memory.

But I'm alone, I think to myself, and then say it aloud, and he, unsurprisingly, tells me to "Shut up. You're walking."

As I walk the mile and a half to school, my pace is fast, I look both ways, and regularly check behind me and to each side. I feel ready to run at any moment I need to, especially if a car slows down near me. Dad says he will drive by with Thomas at one point, but does not say whether he would say "Hi."

I peer into the windows of cars going by. A lot of them look similar to my dad's. Head up high. I feel like Dad wants someone to take me, and it's up to me to protect myself. I will not let myself down, I tell myself through tears and with each step I already feel like I'm already running. I feel relief when I get to school as I sit in the chair I'm assigned. I wonder if anybody else walked as far as I did. Some other kids must walk. It's normal for them and scary for me because it's new, probably.

He never says "Hi," but when I get home from school he shares, "I saw you and didn't want to disturb you. You did a good job. I'm proud of you."

And I try to let the praise soak in, but it falls flat like a damp washcloth to the ground.

— —

I feel curious about being on the student council. It seems like something a good kid would do, so I'm not sure that I qualify, but might as well try. I don't tell anyone about it.

Some people put up signs with their faces on it, and I would never do that. I'll give my speech, and it will speak for itself. I am a qualified candidate to carry out the tasks of Secretary. A teacher asked me why I didn't go for president or vice president, and that never crossed my mind. To be at the lowest level seems like more than enough. And after the results come in, and I don't get it, I wonder if it really was just a popularity contest. Not about merit, but about putting your face on a poster so people know who you are. I wonder if even a single person voted for me. I didn't even vote for myself to show good will. You know, this is too much for me. I decide it isn't for me, and don't try it again.

— —

"When I die, spread my ashes," my dad slurs with a beer in hand, as I listen attentively.

"I don't want to talk about your death, Dad,"

"I'm talking!" He raises a finger... "You can take me to the pyramids, take me to the golden gate bridge, up at Niagara Falls... the mountains, into the water. I want to be everywhere. Promise you'll do it, Stephanie."

I look him in the eye and know I am making a promise I will keep. "I promise."

1998, age 8, Novato, CA

Dear Diary,

Today I went to the zoo. It was really fun just the girls went, Karla, Cassie. Dad came too, but he isn't a girl. Dad told me a secret that Mom wanted the girls to get out of the house so she could wrap our presents. I almost told Karla, but Dad stopped me. I got some cotton candy at the zoo. I got most of it and pink popcorn and tomorrow is Christmas Eve I bet it's going to be fun. I'm just so excited I can't wait!

— —

I can barely keep my eyes open, but it's worth it. It's just before 4am, completely dark out and I'm walking to the car, and

I'm beaming with crusty eyes from a sleep I'd normally continue hours longer.

"The other kids won't do this because they're lazy, but you are different," he says, and I disregard the comparison and focus on the accolades. I'm different. In a good way.

I get up early, not because I have to, but because he wants me to and I'm happy to make him happy. We drive to the police station and he says I can sleep for a couple of hours before set up begins. I do this every year. Putting out Easter eggs at Easter and setting up presents at Christmas. It's "for the poor kids," Dad says. But I don't do it for them if I'm honest. I do it for him. I would lose any amount of sleep if it meant making him smile and he must know it. All I have to do is ignore it when I'm tired or hungry or when I have to use the bathroom. It can wait. What's important is that he knows I'm here for him, no matter what.

Taking pictures of people on Santa's lap and the Easter bunny's lap like he's a springtime Santa. Dad says I have the best steady hand, even better than an adult, so I take the pictures. That I'm so mature and can help people feel happy and calm. He doesn't say the last part, but I know it to be true.

I ask them to smile and see the hope and wonder of the holiday overtake them, and can't help but feel a heavy heart that's light with gratitude for what I have, or at least can have if I deserve it. And since nobody else will get up at that early hour with him, for him, year after year, but me, it's like an unspoken promise.

He talks and I listen, even though he calls me a chatterbox, I know I listen a lot.

2000, age 9, Novato, CA

I'm not allowed to be upstairs. Everybody else's bedroom is upstairs, and mine is downstairs. I feel like this house is haunted at times, and I'm so close to the front door, someone could snatch me. I know a lot of people would like to be alone downstairs. I always did things by myself early: showers and baths when I was five, getting dressed by myself when I was four. Cutting my own nails when I was six after my mom cut them so short my fingertips were bleeding. They try, but I do it all better for myself and they must like not having to take care of me so much. When I do it, the temperature is just right, my clothes look better together, and I cut my nails to the perfect length. The thing is, when I'm not allowed to even walk upstairs when everybody else sleeps there, I feel like I'm not a part of the family. Not welcome. Different. Alone. I know they want to keep a fight or argument from happening.

Dad always says to even Tyler, "Don't like Stephanie. She'll scratch your eyes out!"

Tyler is zero years old, so he doesn't understand yet, but one day he will and he will stop loving me, too. I just want to be allowed to go upstairs.

— —

Each Fall we go to the trees in front of my old preschool where walnuts are on the ground, still in their shells and fleshy outer layer. Sometimes they're hard and green, but when they're soft black and brown is when we can peel them to reveal the shell and leave them outside to dry out and become real crunchy nuts. We don't talk much, my dad and I, but it's quality time. I place them in the bag and he'll give me another one when it's full. It's simple and fun.

— —

Dear Diary,

Today I'm punished but I don't care. I have music! Grease music! Oh yeah, and I can't wait for Auntie Jewel and Evan to come! I made her a really cool poster! It's a picture of her with stuff on it. I think she might be here. I'm going to check. No, not yet, but she will be soon. She said that she'd come 8:00 or 9:00! It's 9:18 now I guess there was some traffic! I hope it wasn't too bad. I really love as in love Auntie Jewel. I got her letter today. Oh no, I mean not today, but on Saint Patrick's Day March 17. I wrote her back right when I got the letter. I gave her some glitter body lotion and a golden ring with hearts on it. I hope she likes it — I think she will. Oh yeah and by the way Jewel got me some bead clips, they are really pretty. I got short jeans today with Mom. They are light blue because I didn't want to get black. They are really neat. I think they are here. It's 9:40. Maybe they are here. She has been here already 'cause Karla came into my room, then she said she'd be down in a few minutes. I dropped the timer and bent down and hurt myself so much I cried and Dad told me to go to my room because I was crying. But Auntie Jewel is in my room now! We read the rest of the chapter of Pippi Longstocking and I sang. I wanted her to tell me witch [sic] song I sang better- hopelessly devoted to you or the worst thing I could say. I sang both of them. She said she liked hopelessly devoted to you! So, she told me to sing again because she had some moves. So, I sang again and she did kinda wacko movements. But I didn't want to hurt her feelings, so I just said one word, they were "great." Oh yeah, and before I forget, Karla gave me red, pink, green, blue, purple, and black markers or crayons all in on [sic] ! It's so cool! I can't wait until my sleepover day out with Auntie Jewel! Stephanie

2000, age 9, Novato, CA

I am 9 years old.

Sitting in my room.

Hunched over my bed.

Bawling my eyes out.

Wondering if life will get better.

Pretty deep in despair.

Which isn't uncommon for me.

But what is WAY less common?

And literally hasn't happened since?

Clear as day.

A friendly female voice cheers in my ear:

"You can be happy now."

What. The. Fuck.

I immediately stop crying.

Shaken by what I am pretty sure I just heard.

Chuckle in my discomfort for a quick second.

I can barely process it.

Until awe quickly turns to anger.

Whatever the hell that just was, is obviously wrong.

All the things going on in my life.

That are totally out of my control.

...And I can STILL be HAPPY?

That disembodied cheerful voice

If it had a face,

I'd have wanted to smack it.

No.

Just, no.

I dismiss that message.

Rattled by its clarity.

2000, age 10, Novato, CA

"Do you want to vote in this election, Stephanie? You can decide on my ballot. You just have to vote for George Bush."

"But what if I want to vote for Al Gore, Dad?"

"Then you don't get to. You can decide and do it right now."

"If I don't really get to choose, you can sign it yourself. Let's not pretend it's my choice if it's actually yours."

"Why do you have to be so difficult? I'll get one of the other kids to do it. You lost your chance." He puffs his chest and speed walks out of the room.

I've always been my grandmas' favorite. All the grandmas. My parents weren't close to their moms or dads, and I'm not close to my mom or dad either, but among all the other kids, my siblings, I can tell that I am the favorite of my grandmas. One even told me and I believe her. How can I be the favorite to my grandmas, and so far from it at home? Are my parents jealous? Am I really the favorite, or are they, my grandmas, happy I'm giving my parents a hard time, like maybe my parents used to give them when they were kids? I don't want to be involved, if that's the case. I just want to be myself.

— —

I recall a time when I was seven, and my mom just helped me with my hair. I sat down on the couch next to my dad, and he asked me a question.

"You know who you look just like?" "Who, Dad?"

"Patty McCormick," he says with a smile. "Who's that?" I ask, curiously.

"She's a girl from the movies. You have the same pigtails.

You act just like her, too. You are just like her."

"Cool, I want to see her. Can you tell me more about her?

What movie is she in? Have I seen it?"

"We haven't seen it yet, but we should, because you are so much like her. The movie is called the Bad Seed."

He continues smiling.

"Dad... is she the main character? What is a bad seed?" "Yes, she's the main character. She's the bad seed. A mean, evil little girl. Everyone thinks she is so nice and sweet, but she does some bad things. Just like you."

I feel myself retract and constrict both with my arms and my insides. "Are you calling me a bad seed?"

"I didn't call you that. I called you Patty McCormick. Do you want to watch it?"

"Oh, I thought you were calling me that, but you didn't actually say it. Yes, I want to see it." I say, uncomfortable but still curious. I want to know why she is bad. And why she is like me.

As I watch the movie, she does seem nice, and her hair is in braids like mine today. And then I see the part where she kills another kid. She does it by not helping him and letting it happen when she could have helped. She set up the whole thing, too. It wasn't an accident.

This is what my dad thinks I'm like. The nice part and the evil part. Why does he think I would do that? I've never been in that situation with a kid, but what you're supposed to do is help them and save them. That's what I think I would do, but I can't prove it. He always calls me "Patty McCormick," which I know means he thinks I'm "bad."

8. STEP RIGHT UP

"She's the same as you, but you refuse to see yourself. She expresses, like a mirror."

- "Villainize" by Stephanie Thoma

1990, age 0

"Step right up, it's your time to make a decision, any decision! Remember me? I'm Jared," a ring-leader-like- character with a big red-lined grin and hair, and a big circus voice announces into the microphone below a spotlight.

Glancing around the poorly lit room, I can hardly make out any details. Within the same instant, lights illuminate onto several mini-stages in front of me.

"Go where you feel drawn," the red-grinned man invites.

I glide over to one of the nearest couples before realizing I'm nothing more than a soft beam of light. No body, no limbs... before I can begin to make sense of the form I'm in, while feeling like I have more-or-less all the other usual aspects of myself, a spotlight jolts onto the two figures I'm nearest and I'm captivated.

A man and woman, bodies of two life-size people, floating on the platform. They're like costumes, all the makings of being alive, yet not alive. They simply need life put into them, I intuit. A woman with a golden blonde bob, a raspberry cardigan, pencil skirt, pearl studs, and kitten heels with fluttering false eyelashes stands beside a man wearing a blue blazer with a deep side part of his short dark brown hair.

"Cincinnati, Ohio... meet Maggie and Jake, here at ages twenty-seven and thirty-four. This is how you'll meet them, anyway. You're looking at a simple, yet comfortable life..."

Then a screen illuminates behind them and shows a three-story house. Cars.

"Emphasis on comfortable." He smirks. "An intact family that is loving and nurturing in the way you need it. You'll do well-enough in school, marry a successful-enough man who loves you *just enough*. Two children who listen to you, so rarely. This is objectively a 'good life' that so many people crave. And it's yours. Guaranteed. Congratulations! You won't live a life that's notable, no fancy awards or going down in history books, but you have had some difficult past lives. If you want a bit of a break — then look. No. Further. Maggie and Jake are going to be lovely parents..."

I feel a sense of dread at this and instinctively pull my orb-of-a-self back and to the right. In that instance, violently, another stage lights up.

Taking notice, Jared chimes, "Okay, okay, you want to see more options? Usually, the first is the way to go, but that's perfectly fine. Moving on..."

Two figures each with brown hair, no pearls, but they're wearing jeans and some plaid...

"Here you have Tom and Jean, 37 and 28. The first half of your life will be significantly more difficult than the second. This is the life where you have the potential to make a name for yourself and even find love. As long as you make it through that first part, that is. It's quite a doozy! Let's just say it's going to be a bit of what you have experienced already in other lives, so it'll be familiar, more "interesting" than good, but you'll be comfortable in other ways, you'll have a roof over your head, enough to eat… big family. You know, we don't have a lot of time here for this one. The window is closing pretty quickly. It's time to make a decision. Or maybe I'll see you in another fifty to one hundred years! I'm not sure what's happening here, but if you don't move forward this instant, it's gone forever. Five, four, three…"

I close my eyes with a different shade of dread as before, but there's something here for me. When I glide forward before I can hear him say "one" I feel my being immersed in water. It's immediately dark and I'm quickly sliding down a tube, like a water-slide, like the inside of a rave bracelet. Deep violet-hued and fast as light — I would scream, but it seems like I don't have that capability yet. It's more of an "oh shit" inner monologue. It's moving faster and faster, the water is filling the space. Can I still breathe? Yes. It feels like I'm flying, but I have no control. The sense of dread is replaced with surrender and depth and quickness and the next moment, everything goes black.

CONCLUSION

Pt I.

My wish is that you feel supported in being your quirky self *and* in connection with others.

It could be in the form of an army of friends who have your back and remind you of who you are when you lose sight of it. But most of all, I want you to not just feel, but *know* how very supported you are in ways you cannot see.

If you find yourself crying alone, I hope you hear a faint "I love you," even if it's in your own voice, in your own head. If you find yourself wondering if it's all worth it, if you can actually do this, please know that it can be and you will.

You may be in a valley and although nobody will be coming to save you, it's not because nobody wants to, it's that nobody truly can.

The perceived lack of saviors is not what matters most in your evolution.

You may be in a valley and although people may be throwing rocks, layering judgments on or misunderstanding how you naturally show up, direct your focus to those extending a branch.

Even if it's one person amongst many, know that the person extending the branch is embodying the truth of humanity. It's also more powerful than the other forces combined.

Let that truth be experienced, wholly.

Life can feel crazy and you don't need to internalize that as a fault of yours, but as an opportunity to explore what comes next, and if you'd try a new approach in a similar situation in the future.

How do you want to feel? Who do you want to be?

You could feel joyful and vibrant and so full of life and energy and vitality. The kind of energy that comes from feeling the sun beaming on your shoulders and face while overlooking a tranquil lake.

You could be a person who decides to be curious instead of judgmental. Compassionate toward others and yourself. Defaulting to the benefit of the doubt, asking for clarity, and forgiveness. To let all of the contemplation turned rumination, go. To be of service, creating things that are meaningful to others while having fun.

To love yourself and those in your orbit with such depth that it invites others to do the same.

Pt II.

What isn't healed can appear like a mirage, distracting us from success, plopping us back into that state of mind. Transmuting pain is what we must do. To experience the spectrum of emotions fully... the bravery it takes to do this.

To open your heart again and again, to become wiser but not bitter with each time it was cradled with care, then carelessly bruised.

To see everything as information, but not fall into the logic trap, because that isn't where magic resides.

You may think once you discover how something works, or why this past event happened, it will be healed. This is not how it works.

Sure, time can heal, but healing can also happen in an instant. Piercing through the film of a reality in which you understand and own the sovereignty in that knowing.

Your perspective and ability to fully feel what is real for you is what will set you free to live as intended.

It's time to normalize letting emotions move through you and inspire real changes in your life if you don't like what you're feeling. Let that movie bring you to tears without understanding why. Let yourself laugh for no good reason. Your brain is a magnificent piece of the broader life puzzle that deserves to be integrated.

Sure, hurt people hurt people, but they also heal us. They also *are* us. Some people provide the yin for the yang to enter and allow you to deepen your gratitude, if only for a chapter of your story, they are all the sweeter, because you have known otherwise. It's not about waiting for certain people to accept and embrace you, but having the courage to accept and embrace yourself no matter what.

BOOK CLUB QUESTIONS

You can select all of the questions, or a few of them, for discussion in a small group of trusted friends, or strangers in one or multiple sessions.

Alternatively, you are welcome to answer these reflection questions privately in a journal.

Personal Identity and Authenticity

1. Do you feel you can be authentic and loved at the same time? Why or why not?
2. Have you ever felt like you were living a double life? One way at home, another way at work or school? What were the archetypes and how did each feel?
3. Were you ever given a label that didn't fit? How did it impact you?
4. In what ways has intentionally being compliant or disconnected from your truth impacted your personal and professional development?
5. How has your sense of identity evolved throughout your life? What experiences or realizations have shaped this evolution?

Relationships and Family Dynamics

1. What type of love relationship pattern do you think a black sheep or scapegoated child is most likely to attract? How

would they feel both healed and betrayed by a romantic relationship with the opposite?

2. In what ways is your taste in romantic partners a reflection of the example a parent set, versus its opposite?

3. What does "family" mean to you?

4. Have you ever felt the need to protect your parents? Keeping some things private, since other people may harshly judge or not understand? Why?

5. How do you define or experience unconditional love? For yourself? For others?

6. How have your family dynamics influenced your approach to conflict resolution in other relationships?

Boundaries and Social Norms

1. What do you think about setting boundaries versus embodying a standard? Walking away with or without discussion?

2. Are there things you would do if they weren't stigmatized by society? What is one of these things, and why do you want to experience it?

3. Do you give people a chance to show you another side of themselves or do you believe gossip you hear? Why or why not?

4. How do you navigate situations where your personal values conflict with societal expectations?

Mental Health and Well-being

1. What are your thoughts on medications as a treatment option for mental health? Should they be used as a last resort or as a part of a holistic treatment plan?

2. Is being delusional a good or bad thing? Why or why not? How do you define delusion?

3. Was there ever a time your reality was questioned? How did it impact you? How did you find your truth?

4. Do you believe in post-traumatic growth, the concept that trying events foster more resilience or empathy? Why or why not?

5. How do you practice self-care and maintain your mental health in challenging times?

Social Justice and Systemic Issues

1. Do you tend to think differently of people who have been incarcerated? Why or why not? Do you question the prison/justice system or apply the fault to the incarcerated?

2. Do you tend to think differently of people who have been checked into a mental institution? Why or why not? Do you question the mental healthcare system or apply the stigma to the institutionalized?

3. If you saw a child being physically reprimanded in public by their caregiver, what would you do? Has this happened? What did you do? What was the aftermath? Or what did you consider doing, but ultimately didn't, and why?

4. In what ways do the mental healthcare and justice systems in your country excel or fall short in their service to individuals and society?

5. How can individuals contribute to positive systemic change in mental healthcare and justice systems?

Philosophical Reflections

1. Is anyone inherently toxic? Why or why not?

2. Would you rather live a life that's good or interesting? Explain your choice.

3. Do you agree that doing the same thing and expecting a different result is a "fool's move"? Specifically, a child acting out defiance? A disciplinarian escalating punishments for the child's behaviors? Why or why not?

4. From your own experiences, do you remember the 'bad things' you did, or the repercussions of those things as a child? Which is clearer in your memory? Why do you think that is?

5. How do you reconcile the tension between personal responsibility and the influence of external circumstances in shaping one's life choices?

CONTACT

Explore Coaching:
   StephanieThoma.com/coaching

Join the Email Community:
   StephanieThoma.com/newsletter

Book Stephanie to Speak (podcasts, conferences & retreats):
   StephanieThoma.com/speaking

Connect on Social Media:
- instagram.com/stephaniemthoma
- facebook.com/stephaniemthoma
- linkedin.com/in/stephaniemthoma
- youtube.com/@stephaniemthoma

Download the original song:
- Spotify, "Villainize" by Stephanie Thoma

ACKNOWLEDGEMENTS

Thank you to each of the characters mentioned in this book. No matter what form our relationship has taken today or how enduring or short our connection has been, I'm grateful for the time we have had to walk alongside one another through this life.

Mom and Dad, you were the best parents for me to learn these lessons and I trust you did the best you could. I am grateful for the interesting life you set the stage for me to lead, scars, gifts and all. I love you both.

First love, you were the ideal introduction to romance, and I feel grateful to have shared that formative experience that I experienced as healing at the time.

Liz Entin, my author friend and the very first person to read this in its roughest, rawest form. You met the draft with such compassion, and thoughtful comments. Your feedback was instrumental in opening the floodgates to sharing these words with more people. Thank you.

Azul Terronez, thank you for our ideation meeting where we uncovered what would become the book title, and Susie Schaefer for laying out what would become key pillars of the story.

To my manuscript auditor, Leah Fletcher, your British humor in the darker moments of the draft perked me up. Your professionalism and attention to detail undoubtedly set the stage for the rest of my editing team to have a tangible place to start.

To my developmental editor, Eve Porinchak, when we first connected it was such a special feeling to know about your advocacy work in justice and its intersection with developmental editing — an invaluable perspective to help shape this story.

To my copy editor Emily LeVault, thanks for your dedication to polishing my words, profound empathy, patience, and being my trusted final set of eyes on this thing.

To my book launch support group of friends and acquaintances, thank you for being there.

To love: thank you for guiding me through my fear. This project has been the most transformative and healing experience of my life (so far) and I can only imagine what comes next.

ABOUT THE AUTHOR

Stephanie Thoma is an author and leadership & life coach known for her approach to building self-acceptance, confidence, and community. Her debut book, *Confident Introvert*, empowers introverts to excel in social and professional settings by embracing their unique strengths. Her latest release, *Not That Sweet*, delves into modern relationships and self-discovery, encouraging readers to embrace authenticity through embodying personal standards, healthy boundary setting and deep self-knowing.

Featured in Forbes, Entrepreneur, and Psychology Today, Stephanie's work blends emotional insight with practical advice. Through online courses, coaching, and signature talks, she helps individuals build social confidence, foster self-acceptance, and create meaningful connections.

www.ingramcontent.com/pod-product-compliance
Lightning Source LLC
Chambersburg PA
CBHW070140080526
44586CB00015B/1775